ENDORSEMENTS FOR CLAUDIA, HER BOOK AND TRAININGS

There are several characteristics that separate Claudia from other business and personal consultants...she has an uncanny ability to get to the heart of the problem—quickly. She is painfully honest in her appraisal of your situation but always remains genuinely concerned.

— **Dr. Victor B. Cline**, Psychologist

Claudia Nelson weaves a true tale of tragedy and triumph, inspiring her reader with the knowledge that they can overcome, that hope is within reach. It's a must read!

— **Richard Paul Evans**, *#1 New York Times* Best selling author of *The Christmas Box and The Walk*

Your work has inspired many, especially me! You are a heck of a sleuth. Claudia Nelson is the best gumshoe vigilante I have ever met...that rare investor who fought back with the same cunning and guile as the con men who victimized her. Others would have walked away—not Nelson. Her 8-year odyssey to bring a master con artist to justice is inspiring and ultimately satisfying. Along the way she corrals fellow fraud victims, the FBI, the Justice Department, and the IRS to see the case through. Nelson weaves religion, psychology, human potential and even quantum mechanics into a narrative that ultimately reveals the art of the con—and why we continue to let ourselves be deceived.

— **Dirk Smillie**, *Forbes* magazine

One of Claudia's greatest skills is her ability to gain the trust of and effectively relate and communicate to people of different ethnic, economic, age and religious backgrounds. People seem to immediately sense her integrity. Whether she speaks to one person or several thousand, she is highly effective.

— **Wally Minto**, Author and Father of *Alpha Awareness Training*

Claudia is extremely intelligent—not only in terms of native intelligence, but because she reflects thoughtfully on her experience. She is very motivated and a very, very hard worker.

— **Lavina Fielding Anderson**, Author and Editor

I have met few students who have the intelligence and ability to absorb the information presented, expand upon it, and use it to achieve such positive results. Yet there are some things that cannot be taught such as intuitive ability, the gift of vision, and the ability to bring a vision into reality. These are probably Claudia's strongest qualities.

— **Dr. Jay Clegg**, Professor of Communication and mentor

I believe what I have been learning in my trainings is more valuable and important than any other knowledge I have obtained. I use this training every day in some way.

— **Jan Blosch**, Student

After going through the course, my attitude towards life has turned around 180 degrees, and my life and business are a thousand times better. Thank You!

— **Doyle Scott**, Student

Thanks to you, every day of my life since the program has been easier, more fun, and my future much brighter!! Thanks again!!

— **Margie Richins**, Student

I would recommend Claudia's workshop to anyone, even if they don't have real big problems. I am looking forward to going through this workshop again with my husband.

— **Julie Turley**, Student

A lovely profound woman with many talents, a loving person to know.

— **Terrance Potthoff**, Student

You are a gift to the Universe.

— **Rev. George Dashiell**, Student

RISING *from* ASHES

Discover Your
HIDDEN POWER
Through Adversity

CLAUDIA T. NELSON

NEW YORK

RISING *from* ASHES
Discover Your HIDDEN POWER *Through Adversity*

by CLAUDIA T. NELSON
© 2011 Claudia T. Nelson. All rights reserved.

ISBN 978-1-60037-996-3 Paperback
ISBN 978-1-60037-997-0 eBook
Library of Congress Control Number: 2011927217

Published by:
MORGAN JAMES PUBLISHING
The Entrepreneurial Publisher
5 Penn Plaza, 23rd Floor
New York City, New York 10001
(212) 655-5470 Office
(516) 908-4496 Fax
www.MorganJamesPublishing.com

Interior Design by:
Bonnie Bushman
bbushman@bresnan.net

In an effort to support local communities, raise awareness and funds, Morgan James Publishing donates one percent of all book sales for the life of each book to Habitat for Humanity.
Get involved today, visit
www.HelpHabitatForHumanity.org.

About the Book Cover

THE PHOENIX BIRD LEGEND

The version of the Phoenix on the book cover was drawn by Susan Pettit who received it in a dream, after triumphantly rising from the ashes of her former life. The legend of the Phoenix Bird has been around for centuries with several variations of the legend and the bird.

The basic version: The Phoenix Bird is a supernatural creature that lives for 1,000 years, then builds its own funeral pyre and throws itself into the flames. As it dies, it is reborn anew and rises from the ashes to live another 1,000 years.

Symbolically, the Phoenix is a metaphor for our lives.

Seldom do our lives go as planned. We don't consciously throw ourselves into flames and say, "It's time to die and be born anew." It simply happens. Old relationships, dreams, jobs and plans for our future do die and burn to ashes. Sometimes we feel we can't go on, that life is over.

Life as we knew it is over. That's what the death of the Phoenix symbolizes. But we, like the Phoenix, can rise from the ashes of our old life and be reborn into a new and better one. This is:

"The Phoenix Principle"

This book shows you how to seize the Phoenix Opportunity to find new life, finding hope when hope has been lost.

This book will allow you to see things you've never seen or understood before. You will never need another self-help book if you apply the principles found in *Rising from Ashes*.

DISCLAIMER

This is not the ordinary self-help book.

Rising from Ashes refused to be a bandage to cover a psychic wound. Instead, it chose to be a Roto-Rooter and dig out the root of the wound.

The root is, you've forgotten who you really are.

The real you *is perfect and powerful and needs no change.*

Rising from Ashes helps you *remember* the *real* you by Roto-Rooting out what is *not* you.

The stories it contains, which show you the difference between the fake you and real you, are sensitive. Therefore, some names, details and circumstances have been altered.

ACKNOWLEDGMENTS

This book has been one of the most challenging things I have ever undertaken, and it would not have been possible without the support, generosity, and patience of many friends and associates. It is the culmination of over a half-century of experience, life-changing inspiration, and life-challenging frustration. All this has given me the opportunity to accomplish what I've known that I came here to do since I was sixteen years old. At age sixteen, I was given a spiritual blessing in which I was told I would face many adversities in my life and that I would have the knowledge, understanding, wisdom, and courage to overcome them all. These experiences would help me serve my purpose well: to raise others to a higher plane of living.

I feel a deep sense of gratitude to all who showed up at just the right time to offer the assistance and guidance that was needed at that moment:

To my husband and children who have endured the time I spent at the computer writing this book, instead of with them.

To my wonderful editors Jude Anson, Jan Werner, and Marla Markman who went more than the extra mile in getting this book ready for publication.

To my computer guru, Keith Couch, who kept me sane through all my computer problems, offered editorial suggestions, and generously shared his talents as a photographer. My signature photograph is his work.

To my illustrator, Susan Pettit, who provided illustrations for the book and who dreamed and drew the original Phoenix for the cover, which Mark Kozak developed into a wonderful book cover in record time to meet a deadline.

To my old college friend, Grant Fairbanks, M.D., for his amazing two-minute sketch of the human Phoenix. He is not only a wonderful artist with pen and paint, he has used his amazing artistic ability to become one of the nation's leading plastic surgeons.

To my physicist friend, Susanne Gallivan, whose guidance helped me take complex quantum-physics concepts and keep them accurate while making them simple.

To Scott Frishman, Dave Holland, Bonnie Burroughs, Karla Briggs, Darla Manwill, Linae Tiede, Jerry Hopkins and Hal, who all made valuable contributions with their insights and suggestions for the book.

To my father, mother, and sister for the lessons they taught and whose tragic deaths forced me to move into a higher plane of living to survive the pain of their loss.

To my publishing team at Morgan James, Margo Toulouse, David Hancock, Jim Howard and Rick Frishman, for their wonderful team effort in publishing and promoting this book, and to Bonnie Bushman for her outstanding book design.

TABLE OF CONTENTS

Section One
AN (OPEN) GUT VIEW
OF THE EGO WORLD

The best-selling book ever written (the Bible) tells us that the only way to achieve freedom from the ego is to understand the pain and suffering that the ego itself is causing.

—**Rabbi Michael Berg**, author of Well of Life

PROLOGUE

The seeds for this book were planted three days before Christmas in the winter of 1990. On that day, years of domino traumas and unrelenting pain began for my family and me. I discovered on that day, from the deepest recesses of my soul, how it felt to be brutally victimized.

Even through this miasma of pain and desperation I made a decision: I would not allow this to ruin my life. I would find a way to recover and become whole again. My life would then be about helping other victims.

After recovering sufficiently from my own trauma, I began working in the courts creating workshops and seminars for those who were victimizing themselves with alcohol and drugs assisting them in alleviating their suffering and turning their lives around. I also worked with perpetrators of serious crime who had victimized themselves by harming others. It was very gratifying to watch them struggle through their own repentance process and become whole.

Never could I have envisioned that I'd be victimized again ten years later—this time in an international Ponzi scheme. But this time it couldn't shake me to the core. I had my *victim- to-victor* formula down pat. It empowered me not only to recover but also to be a major force in exposing and bringing the con men to justice.

While the seeds for this book were planted in 1990, they began to sprout in the spring of 2005 when I received a call from Dirk Smillie, a senior fraud writer from *Forbes* magazine. He'd discovered my name in a newspaper article, reporting that Dennis D. Cope and Edgar Bias had been indicted in an international Ponzi scheme. I was their victim, the first to discover Cope was a fraud and report it to the authorities, and then pursue the case for eight years until the fraudsters were put in prison.

As I pulled up victim stories for Smillie's article, stories I'd gathered for the prosecution, I was again overwhelmed with the anguish Cope and Bias left in their wake…for thousands of victims. Sitting in the middle of the floor in my office, file folders strewn around me, victim stories in hand, I closed my eyes, and felt an overwhelming desire for someone to do something to help the victims.

Just then the phone rang. It was one of my most trusted and "in tune" friends, Maureen St. Germain. I began unloading my feelings, explaining all the pain and trauma these Ponzi victims had suffered. The words just came flooding out, as if my mouth were a dam that finally cracked after holding back tons of water pressure for too many years. The words just exploded out: "Maureen, someone has to help these victims!"

"It's you, Claudia, you'll write a book that will help." Her words were gentle, yet held an uncanny power.

Being in the middle of writing *Murder, Death and Rebirth*, a book to help victims, I had no desire to be "the one," at least not now. After tossing and turning all night, I knew in my heart Maureen was right, yet passionately wished she were wrong. *Murder, Death and Rebirth* had to be put on the shelf until later.

This book is the result, a six-year undertaking. I wrote several versions before it felt right. Before it felt right, I had to allow it to take on its own life and become what it wanted to become. "I don't know what I expected it to become, but this isn't it."

Although I began the book to help victims avoid and/or recover from the effects of fraud, it became clear the book had a bigger purpose. It wanted to provide principles that would work for anyone who had suffered any kind of adversity, and, as you will discover, the book, with a force of its own, decided to bring you an even greater message.

The book is unusual. It turned out to be both entertaining and informative—and transformative.

For those who want to be *entertained* by true stories of mystery, intrigue, and how the power of the human spirit can triumph over tragedy, you'll enjoy it on that level. Yet those who have previewed the book looking for entertainment were surprised to experience transformative insights, which continued even after they'd finished the book.

For those who want to be *informed* of the scientific and metaphysical principles behind how to triumph over tragedy, you'll find that too. Here, too, while reading for information, you may be surprised to experience transformative insights.

For those who have a burning desire to apply the principles to overcome adversity, be *transformed* and create the life you've always desired, that's here too.

To experience transformation, you might need to read this book more than once. Keep it by your side. Refer to it often. Begin practicing the kind of thinking and behaviors found in **Section Two.** Work to perfect them, one at a time. The more you practice, the faster you will awaken to who you really are—an incredibly talented, intelligent, powerful being. Once you are connected to the *real* you, you will never again be vulnerable to con men or any other abuser. You will become the victor, never again the victim.

As you become more connected to whom you really are, you will be in greater vibrational alignment with the powerful information in **Section Three.** You will then be able to use it effectively to further enhance your life.

To those of you who already fully understand and are readily able to use all this information, CONGRATULATIONS!

While this book began with a phone call from Dirk Smillie, from *Forbes* magazine, how it ends is up to you.

Introduction

THE WORLDS WE LIVE IN

We can't solve the significant problems we face with the
same level of thinking we were at when we created them.
—Nobel prize winner, **Albert Einstein**

A young father and his five year old son were in a department store at Christmas time observing an inflatable life-sized Santa. A teenage boy walked over to the Santa, punched him and tipped him over. The Santa popped right back up. After watching this happen several times, the father said to his son, "Why do you think that Santa never stays down but keeps popping back up?"

The young boy thought for a minute and said, "I guess it's because he can stand up on the inside." Ahh, the wisdom of a child. When we can stand up on the inside, nothing can keep us down.

As my author/rancher friend put it, "It ain't tippin over that counts ... it is how ya get back up!" —Reid Rosenthall, author of *Threads West.*

This book is about "how ya get back up" once you've been tipped over. But before we can teach you to stand up on the inside, we must challenge your thinking. By embracing the challenge to see differently, you will discover that you have the ability to "get back up" after any blow and still create the kind of life you desire, for this book shows you how you can control your world with your thoughts. You've probably heard that before but never understood how that simple statement impacts your life.

A Course in Miracles tells us that "Few appreciate the real power of the mind, and no one remains fully aware of it all the time. The mind is very powerful and never loses its creative force. It never sleeps. Every instant it is creating. It is hard to recognize that thought and belief combine into a power surge that can literally move mountains…There are no idle thoughts. All thinking produces form at some level."

We have two distinct thought systems. Each has its own personality, its own thought system, its own belief system, and its own agenda. You'll learn how each thought system works and how to control each of them to create your desires.

When we get to the right thought system, we'll understand that all the abilities we have now are only shadows of our real strength.

Before we entered planet earth, our minds were not split. When we gained a body, our mind split into two thought systems so we could experience opposites, the dark, the light, the negative and positive. Only then could we exercise choice, which is a component part of free agency. Our problem-creating thought system is based on fear; our problem-solving thought system is based on love.

So how do we get from fear to love? The principles are simple; perfecting them takes time. *As you digest, practice, and use what you'll learn, the love door will begin to open. And behind these doors you'll find everything you need to bring you peace, prosperity and soooo much more.*

It took a boatload of adversity, which included losing my mother and sister to murder and losing my life savings in a Ponzi scheme, to understand what I'm about to share. Some family members turned to alcohol and drugs, after the murders, to cope. Some Ponzi victims committed suicide or remained victims; others lost marriages, their homes, and their sanity.

By coming to understand Einstein's levels of thought, and learning how to get from one level to the other, I survived the adversity and learned to thrive in spite of it. In this book you will find my secrets.

Although I'd been caught in the wrong thought system when all this adversity occurred, it didn't mean I had to stay there. By choosing to believe that a minus can be made into a plus with just one extra stroke, *I "stroked" an approach to life that helped me and can help you survive and thrive from the worst of what life brings, whether on the home front, the work front, or an economic crisis.*

First step: Make a decision. Do you *intend to remain a victim of your circumstances, or do you intend to become a victor over them?* By choosing to become a victor you are choosing to step out of your fears. To step out of fear, you must be willing to see things differently.

How many times have your eyes or ears deceived you?

Brain scientist Dr. Jill Bolte Taylor gives a scientific reason things are not always as they seem and why our senses deceive us:

"Sensory information streams in through our sensory systems and is immediately processed through the limbic system."

She explains further that all sensory information passes through the fear center of the limbic system, the amygdala, which flags any present situation as dangerous if it perceives it is anything like something that has happened in the past that seemed to be dangerous.

A good example would be a veteran who has served in battle and suffers from Post Traumatic Stress Syndrome. If he hears a car backfire, he dives under a table because it sounds like a gun. Our senses deceive us because the information they provide is based on fear. They will tell you safe is dangerous and dangerous is safe. In Debbie's story you'll see how her sensory input told her something was safe when it was extremely dangerous.

Anything processed through our fear thought system is contaminated and becomes unreliable, limiting, and even…dangerous. We need to learn to think from a more reliable thought system to become the victor.

Here's an overview of the two worlds of thought:

Problem-Creating Thought System	Problem-Solving Thought System
The 1% World	The 99% World
• We experience spiritual darkness and confusion.	• We are surrounded by order, perfection and light.
• We are caught up in the ego world— never feeling good enough.	• We are confident and humble.
• We are victims of circumstances and have no control.	• We are victors with total control.
• We feel empty, unfulfilled, turn to addictions.	• We are fulfilled in the *genuine* us.
• We unconsciously create what we don't want.	• We consciously create what we desire.
• There is no hope for permanent, positive change.	• We can create permanent, positive, lasting change.
• We create problems.	• We solve problems.
• Our fear-based thought system rules.	• Our love-based thought system takes over.
• Pain is dominant.	• Peace reigns.

Another huge difference between the two worlds is this: In our 1% world, we are obsessed with getting for ourselves alone. In our 99% world, we focus on giving. We understand that giving with the right attitude is really giving to ourselves; we understand giving is an act of love and takes us to, and keeps us connected to, our 99% world; we understand that giving helps us remember who we really are; we understand that giving quiets our ego and brings us peace. There are so many ways to give. We can share our time, talents, wisdom, kindness or our resources, to name a few.

While developing this survive and thrive process through struggle, trial and exploring many thought systems, I discovered the techniques that will move us out of the darkness of our fear-based thought system into the light where we make contact with our internal guru (*gu* means darkness; *ru* means light).

In Sections One and Two, you will find poignant stories to facilitate you in your search for your own internal guru. The stories are exciting, inspirational, sometimes harrowing, but always educational. It is my hope and prayer that this book will be a shortcut that allows you to find your guru without having to experience the difficult times I experienced.

This book is a journey of discovering the truths that set you free and how adversity becomes a catalyst, alerting you that it is time for your journey to begin.

What do I mean by "setting you free"? I mean to be free of your in-the-box thinking that keeps you in fear, stuck and limited, free to find and embrace who you really are, free to know what you are destined to achieve, free to know and do unencumbered by fears and doubts. Are any of you that free yet?

Who are you really? Buckminster Fuller, father of the geodesic dome, says that you are a genius. He says,

"We all come into life as geniuses...but life de-geniuses us."

It is my hope that you will use this book to *re-genius* yourself.

We all have a special kind of genius within us that will allow us to accomplish whatever we were intended to accomplish. This book is designed to take you from this thinking world of doubt and fear, this place of...I want to, but can't... to the place of freedom where all knowledge is available and all doubts are gone. This is the place you'll find your guru, your genius and your purpose, and the courage to fulfill that purpose. It's the place of...I can and I will.

By shedding your old thoughts, your too-tight skin that is strangling you and by dumping your baggage, you'll find that place. By doing this, you're doing something remarkable—in addition to helping yourself, you are helping an astonishing number of other people in ways you do not yet begin to understand. How did I learn what I'll be sharing? Most of it came from my experiences, as told by my biographer...

Claudia Nelson, Woman of Unconventional Courage

By Doris Gallan

Claudia's conservative upbringing did little to prepare her for the violence and loss she has experienced in her life. Brought up to unquestioningly accept the wisdom of her elders and to place her fate in the hands of others, it took accidents, crime and health issues to wake her up and take control of her life and to understand she couldn't survive all she faced by continuing to live in the world of thought others had created for her.

She began questioning the conventions of her society and her programming; she sought answers to questions that shouldn't be asked. From an early age Claudia viewed the world differently than those around her; but wanting to fit in, she kept those thoughts to herself.

A deep thirst for knowledge possessed her, driving her to study strange practices and religions in foreign lands.

Having more daunting personal experiences than any one human should be burdened with, her indefatigable curiosity about how others view the world, without blindly accepting their ideas as her own, built the strength needed to transform herself from a victim into a victor, then help others do the same.

Where Tradition Met the Unconventional

The path-finding gene runs deep in Claudia, as her ancestors were Mormon pioneers whose forefathers came to America in the 1600s after giving up everything to pursue freedom and opportunity. From them, Claudia inherited the pioneering spirit to find a new freedom for herself and others victimized and imprisoned in their own limited world of "in-the-box thinking."

Except for the tragic death of her father in an automobile accident while she was away enjoying her honeymoon, Claudia's life flowed much as that of any conservative Christian. After being raised in the small mining town of Ely, Nevada, she went to college, married, had eight children, and kept busy raising children and writing religious lessons for the women and youth of her worldwide church.

But she always felt like a butterfly in a box, her spirit reaching for more connection to the ultimate Truth. In a dream, she was told that to obtain this truth she needed to look for ways to see life from different angles, thus validating the words of French philosopher, Emile Chartier:

"Nothing is more dangerous than an idea when it is the only one you have."

But it was personal experience that gave Claudia her most important education. In 1990, her mother and sister were murdered in their mountain cabin, ironically called Tiede's Tranquility. This, and the devastating aftermath of family disintegration and divorce, caused Claudia to experience a heart-wrenching pain for which no outlet could be found. It proved to be the breaking point in a life of blind acceptance.

Programmed to be a victim, to accept her fate and place her faith in God's hands, she decided that wasn't good enough. Instead, she turned her tragedy into a vehicle of assistance for others. She created a registered non-profit organization to create safer communities for families. She never again allowed others to do her thinking for her.

After being diagnosed with cancer, Claudia embarked on what was perhaps her most difficult lesson yet. This would be one to take her through the inner workings of her own soul to become yet another type of survivor and through which she found and cleansed the thought demons that held her hostage to illness.

Unfortunately, the tragedies in her life weren't over. Claudia, her husband, and many others became victims of an enormous Ponzi scheme, which robbed them of their life savings. Sensing that little would be done to the perpetrators unless she took action, she began an eight-year campaign to uncover and provide enough evidence to the FBI and the courts to put the con artists in prison where they couldn't defraud others. Her reputation as a gumshoe-detective vigilante was sealed, thanks to the work she and her "deep throat" source accomplished, which enabled her to support the victims and prevent future victims.

In her search to find ways to protect others and put the criminals in jail, Claudia experienced a number of dramatic encounters. The mafia approached her with an offer difficult to refuse. She was given a "death warning" while pursuing the con men. Despite this warning, she decided she'd rather go out helping someone than retire in a rocking chair. Besides, she figured, her story had hit the media, beginning with a *Forbes* magazine exposé, so she hoped she was now a bit too high profile to kill.

In fact, Dirk Smillie, senior writer at *Forbes* magazine, said,

"Claudia Nelson is the best gumshoe vigilante I have ever met..."

Any one of the tragedies in her life would have felled a lesser person: the violent death of her father, the even more violent murder of her mother and sister, a bout with cancer, a divorce after thirty-two years of marriage, and eight children, and the loss of her life savings in a swindle. Claudia, like many others, was faced with the decision of folding in the face of adversity, fighting and winning, or jumping over obstacles to win. But, in her unique way, this victor found a way to walk—not around, over or under—but through these obstacles. These tragedies have given her ample opportunities to personally test her methods of turning victims into victors. She uses her own life, which explodes with contradictions, to help others make sense of theirs.

But before she could help other victims become victors, Claudia undertook her own journey of exploration, entering territory seldom explored by conservative Christians. Her search for ways to see things differently took her to the jungles of Peru to study with spiritual leaders and to the deep canyons of the Sierra Madres, working with the Huichol Indians. Her journey of contradiction continued as she hiked with and interviewed a group of nudist women and their nudist, Christian minister husbands to see how they thought and was given a book by one of the ministers who wrote it to justify nudity through the *Bible*. She then studied in a Hindu Ashram to understand their thought processes.

Wanting to understand the thoughts of Satanists without facing the danger of joining a coven, she studied a doctoral thesis containing the writings of those who had interviewed Satanists. She then entered the inner world of the mystics and participated in Native American sweat lodges.

Finally, she attended a liberal arts school in the eastern United States, located on a Civil War battleground, where her fellow students encountered the ghosts of Civil War soldiers. Here she studied quantum physics, art and psychology, and ultimately obtained her degree in writing and literature.

It took Claudia many years to learn to become empowered through her own adversities. She now helps others do the same. Her seminars have taken her from prisons to courts to the offices of corporate executives and have helped transform lives.

Her passion is to see people become self-empowered and at peace, as she knows our "out there" world is only a reflection of our "in here" world of thought. As Gandhi said: "Be the change you want to see in the world."

That's Claudia's passion—to help you rid yourself of the *fake and fearful* you that keeps you stuck in your box of limited thinking and help you discover the *real perfect* you where all truth, power, abundance, and peace lies. When enough of us do this, we will finally have world peace.

How the Book Is Structured

My distinctive approach to this book, which came from a dream, isn't a popular one with editors and publishers. My insistence on the holographic approach (looking at a subject from many angles) isn't clear enough for publishers. They're not certain what category this book belongs in. Is it philosophy, spirituality, or science? Is it a memoir or a self-help book?

Frankly, I wondered why a book that explains how to get out of the box needs to belong in one box! But trying to play the game, I explained that the book fits into all the categories. It is the book that will enable people to get where they want to go. It is self-help and a personal empowerment book.

To prepare for the journey ahead, here's a breakdown of the book's structure:

Section One

The world we call real, the one we access with our five senses, we'll call the 1% world, for it is where you find only 1% of truth. This is the world we enter in Section One.

In this world, people never feel they *are* enough because they don't *have* enough. "Enough" is never enough to make them feel secure. They don't know their security is not in their bank account, that their self-worth and net worth are not the same. They develop an addiction to *more*—usually more money. It's a lose/lose world. It is life on a gerbil wheel, always running, never arriving anywhere. This is the world in which our Ponzi story takes place.

The Ponzi story begins with the drama of the courtroom scene; next you get the back-story, explaining everything that happened to get us there; finally I will share the lessons and insights learned over the eight years of pursuing the con men.

Section Two

The other world, your guru world, we'll call the 99% world for that is where you find 99% of truth, the truth that sets us free. This is the world we enter in Section Two.

I know you are worth so much more than you think you are; the world described in Section One is not a world for you. You will find all you are worthy of in your 99% world, the one which we seek, the one which contains the real you. It's a world where fear gives way to love, judgment yields to acceptance, stress fades to peace, and lack dissolves in abundance.

This is the world you'll experience through the stories in Section Two, where you'll find living examples of the beautiful world this love-based 99% world creates. A different principle will be taught with each story, a principle about how we can move from our confusing 1% world of thought to our 99% world where we find our real kingly and queenly guru selves.

Section Three

The third section goes into more academic detail about the process of this journey. It reveals more about the underlying principles at work that can move us from victims to victors and beyond. It is a more complex section, so you'll need to be prepared to put in the work to get the benefit. It will be especially useful for those who want to understand why things work as they do.

I know your journey is important for more than just you. For if things are ever going to change out there in the world, they have to change in our internal worlds first. For "out there" is only a reflection of what is going on in our "in here" world. If enough of us make the journey, our outside world will have to change.

Appendix

Found at www.RisingFromAshes.net Code: *rising.*

To keep this book at a manageable length, I've posted source material and other information on my website that will take intellectually curious readers deeper into some of the more important concepts we cover.

Here you will find several articles that analyze some of the book's topics in more depth.

- *Special Report: Are You the Next Target of a Con Artist?* This explains the kind of people who are likely to be conned, how to avoid remaining a victim if you have been conned, the psychological symptoms victims experience, how con men do their work, and more on how to avoid being cheated.

- *How to Avoid the Nations Top Scams* Federal prosecutors tell us that con men are getting more clever and devious than ever before and play upon time-tested rip-offs with a new twist that cruelly capitalizes on people's current financial distress. Here are the scams that most bedeviled consumers in 2010 and, which, if we're not alert, are likely to rip us off in 2011—if we don't take steps to avoid them.

- *Analysis of Nathaniel Hawthorne's short story "The Birthmark":* This is included for because it is a sophisticated story of how people who think they are in love are often caught in a relationship addiction, how those addicted learn to con to feed that addiction, and how they damage the marriage and themselves. This error of confusing love with addiction and the con artists it produces is more common than we'd like to believe.

- *Analysis of the Language of Good and Evil:* This rare information comes from a yet-to-be-published doctoral thesis of Patty Karamesines. Much of what was learned came from interviews with Satan worshippers and how they suck victims into their covens. Here you will more clearly see how con men use this same language to suck us into their fraud schemes.

— This is my story. Because you are reading it, maybe some of it is your story, too.

We are now entering the 1% world where our Ponzi scheme took place at:

1,000 Poor Me Place

United Kingdom of Suffering, Zip 66666

The world we call real is defined by:
Heart attacks, panic attacks and ozone cracks
Homicide, suicide and genocide
And airplane crashes, stock market crashes and ethnic clashes
High school shootings and religious feuding
And recessions, depressions, and therapy sessions
Family welfare and chemical warfare
And unemployment and missile deployments
Persecution and execution
And massive layoffs and political payoffs
Earthquakes and poisoned lakes
Illness and loneliness
And pain and illegal gain,
Abuses and excuses
Then there are all the things that don't rhyme like
Disease
Money addiction
And psychic vampires *

*Poem revised by author, from *Yehuda Berg's* original in *The Power of Kabbalah*

Chapter One

I'VE BEEN CONNED!

Each friend [and experience] represents a world in us,
a world possibly not born until they arrive, and it is
only by this meeting that a new world is born.
—Writer **Anaïs Nin**

I remember the moment I realized…I'd been conned. I can still feel the feelings. I'm standing in the doorway of my office feeling like someone had suddenly drained my entire body of blood and replaced it with ice water. My skin feels cold and clammy and I'm disoriented, as if I were moving into another dimension of reality to escape the pain of this one. I had become a statistic. It happened because I met a man, a con man that is, by the name of Dennis D. Cope and a new world was born…although not one of my conscious choosing.

I learned from an Associated Press study that in 2009, Americans were cheated out of $16.5 billion in some sort of scheme. With approximately 300 million people in the United States, that translates into one in every eighteen Americans. Since Bernie Madoff, one particular type of scam—the Ponzi scheme—has become a household word. That became blatantly clear when I took my grandkids to the sweet shop and found a tiny package of peppermint gum that contained two little gum squares; on the box was a good-looking shirtless guy with these words over his chest: "Ask me about my Ponzi scheme."

Here I am to tell you about mine. I share it as a learning experience to help you avoid anything similar, or help you recover if you've already been caught in a scam. But most of all I share it because what I learned through it can change your life for the better and help you discover who you really are, as it did for me.

As I dealt with the fallout from my entanglement with a Ponzi scheme, I envied those who could just cry over their loss. I never allowed myself that luxury. Within minutes of that moment in the doorway, I had pulled myself together and took action. They weren't going to get away with this! The decisions I made at that moment made this book possible.

It was one of those turning points in life that alters your destiny, a turning point that would give birth to a whole new world, one that awakened me to a whole new perspective of life, new people and new possibilities.

We'll begin the story three years after the day I had the chilling recognition I had been conned. We'll begin with my courtroom encounter with my con man. After that court scene, I'll share the back-story and reveal answers to questions, such as why are con men so successful? What is the unseen damage they do? Did we fight back? The final chapters of this section will reveal the life-changing lessons and insights gained from the experience.

The story opens in the Sandra Day O'Conner federal courthouse in Phoenix, Arizona, where I'd gone to witness a low moment in the life of Dennis D. Cope, my own personal psychic vampire (one who lives by preying on others). Cope was about to be indicted on thirty-two counts of fraud and money laundering for engineering the Ponzi scheme that robbed me of my life savings.

Rushing through the streets of downtown Phoenix in my nylons, I arrive at the front door of the courthouse at 9 a.m. sharp. Bending over to put on my heels, I notice a wide run crawling up my leg. I ignore it and stare at the awesome glass structure; it seemed to be calling out to all would-be criminals, "Beware, we see you! Commit a crime and you'll end up in this courthouse feeling like you're living in a fishbowl, and you will be."

Security takes forever, and they seize my purse and camera. I'm frustrated because I'm late and start to argue but realize that would just take more time. I rush to the second-floor balcony, which all the courtrooms open onto. It is 9:10 a.m.

The courtrooms are hidden behind closed doors. Clustered around one door is a group of people, none of whom I recognize. One tall, well-built olive-skinned gentleman is leaning against the wall.

A sinking feeling sets in; I'm afraid our case has already begun behind one of those closed doors. Had I flown all this way to arrive just in time to miss the big moment? The thought horrified me.

Another group of people standing by the balcony railing catches my eye; one of them is leaning over the rail, while several people gather around him. I'll check them out; maybe some of them belonged to our case.

I approach the group; a sea of dark, drab suits and dresses. At 5'11" in 3-inch heels, wearing an ankle-length tangerine linen dress and stress-frosted hair, I immediately catch their attention. I ask several individuals on the outside of the cluster whether they are connected with the Cope case. They are not. They're waiting for another case to conclude.

Heaving a sigh of relief, I turn and again notice the group standing next to the courtroom doors and the handsome black man nearby. I begin my trek back across the long, wide hallway. Since I'm the only victim there, it's up to me to gather information. Who is here representing our case? Who is the opposition? I'm about to find out.

And I'm about to meet in flesh and blood our Vampire SWAT (Special Wisdom and Techniques) team. These are the government officials, state and national, who'd worked with me to put Cope away. For the past three years, I've known them only as voices on the phone as we worked together to put Cope behind bars. Later I'll describe them in more detail. For now, all you need to know is they were there to witness this event.

As I'm talking to one of the SWAT team members, I happen to glance over at the other group clustered by the rail, the one I'd approached first. They all break away from the railing and begin walking down the huge corridors towards the elevators. As they moved away, three lone figures stand revealed, huddled against the railing.

Chapter Two

THE INVISIBLE FORCE

If all hearts were open and all desires known as they would be if people showed their souls, how many gapping, sightings, clenched fists, knotted brows, broad grins, and red eyes should we see…
—Author **Thomas Hardy**

That moment of spotting the trio became, for me, a powerful reminder that we're all vulnerable behind our masks of self-confidence.

The smaller of the two men, wearing a dark business suit, scans the first floor as though making mental notes of everyone who entered. A tall, overweight woman wearing a tight-fitting skirt and blouse stands beside him, her dishwater blonde hair severely pulled back from her face and fastened in a bun. Next to her stands a heavyset oval-shaped man with curly black neck-length hair who is also dressed in a dark business suit.

Suddenly, the man leaning over the rail straightens himself and looks in my direction. Could it be? Oh my gosh…it is! Denny Cope—and his wife, Dana! The oval-shaped man had to be Cope's high-priced attorney! The once-handsome and charming Cope, the con, and his once-beautiful wife, Dana, look terrible. Pangs of compassion engulf me. They look so very different than the charming golden couple I'd last seen three years ago.

Our last encounter took place in a beautiful, peaceful setting at the Hyatt Hotel in Scottsdale, Arizona. By that time, the promised return on our investment had never appeared. Cope always had an excuse, but many of the investors were becoming suspicious. My husband and I invited the Copes to dinner, thinking that if we got them alone without the adoring fans, the real Dennis Cope and his true intentions might reveal themselves. I wanted to give him every opportunity to redeem himself before I went to the attorney general in Phoenix.

Denny graciously accepted the invitation, but he brought along his sidekick, Dan Echols, and Dan's wife. If we got Cope to slip up and tell us the truth, he could deny it and Dan would be his witness. Still, getting him with only two adoring fans would still be an improvement over the usual crowd.

Arriving at the parking lot of the Hyatt, we see Cope and group pull in and park a few cars away from ours. Denny and Dana get out of the car, he with his stately presence and good looks and she with her long blonde wavy hair, pleasant face and sexy figure. They looked as if they were stepping right out of a fashion magazine, a gorgeous couple who would stand out in any crowd. Dan and his wife, although pleasant and wholesome-looking, just couldn't compare.

Despite our suspicions, the evening turns into an entertaining meal with friends. The evening is so pleasant I hardly mind getting nothing of substance from Denny— except he does admit he's bought a golf course, then proceeds to justify it. I realize he's actually exposed one of his money-laundering schemes.

When it comes time to pay, Denny grabs the bill before I can.

"But we invited you out; we should pay the bill," I protest.

Charming as ever, he won't have it; we finally succumb. Cope pays.

At that moment, though, something odd happens that I again dismiss. When he sees the amount of the bill, Cope looks a little surprised. He turns his shoulder to us as he pulls out his wallet and thumbs through, as though concerned he doesn't have enough money. Then Dana turns away from us and goes through her purse for more cash. All the time I wonder, "Why doesn't he just use a credit card like everyone else does?"

Still, I remember that beautiful evening we spent together and what a striking and charming couple the Copes made. With that image still in my head, it was shocking to see them now.

Observing Cope

Why is Cope now leaning over the rail looking at the floor below? Is he thinking of jumping? Ending it all by smashing himself on the marble floor below? Is he looking to see how many other victims would show up?

He appears smaller than I had remembered. His brown hair, once dyed with a flamboyant tint of red, is now a dull and lifeless brown. Patches of dye on his skin near the hairline reveal his secret. "It's a cheap home dye job," I'm thinking. "Designed to con the judge, to make him feel sorry for Cope, that he can't even afford to have a professional dye job." A master con man knows all the subtle nuances of his trade, and he uses them to deceive smart, successful people to get what he wants.

I stare at him for a long time and as I register all the changes in him, I think, "There stands a hurting man." It's almost as if a tiny portion of the accumulated pain he's inflicted on thousands of victims had broken loose and found its way back to its rightful owner. Looking at his lifeless face, I realize I'm seeing a human whose dark deeds are reflected in the dark aura that surrounds him, visible to anyone. Even the light streaming through the glass walls of the building can't obscure that sensation of darkness that surrounds him. Then I feel something I can only describe as a mixture of compassion mixed with satisfaction…we had him! We'd stopped his rampage of serial destruction. Universal law had remained constant, and what I described to my children as the "law of the boomerang" (what you put out comes back) had again proven itself. Yet Cope's shrunken body and shriveled soul caused compassion to tug at my senses.

The Invisible Force

Suddenly I feel an invisible phantom-like force push me from behind. I find my legs carrying me across the balcony towards Cope, where he and his wife Dana still stand, leaning against the rail. I think, "What is happening? What am I doing? Yikes! I'm about to come face to face with this…this…this destroyer of lives, this psychic vampire! What will I do? What will I say?"

Cope and I lock eyes, but I detect no emotion in the connection. As I stand there staring at the startling changes in this man, I have to remind myself that this is the man who has destroyed hundreds, even thousands of lives, and that some of his victims even committed suicide. I suspect other victims wished their value systems had allowed them to do the same.

I extend my hand to shake his. His upper arm remains pressed to his side and only his lower arm, from elbow to hand, pops up. He shakes my hand. To be more accurate, he allows me to shake his hand. His face shows no sign of emotion. He just stares at me with stone cold eyes. I feel the deadness—the total lack of emotion—that lurks behind the stare.

I return the look with much softer eyes and say, "I'm sorry it has come to this, Denny. I want you to know it's nothing personal."

Still no emotion…no response. It feels as though I am interacting with a robot or someone highly medicated. He glares at me without uttering a word, as if I'm the guilty party, the criminal.

My mind suddenly flashes back to my college years and Sociology 101. My redheaded professor stands in front of the blackboard lecturing on psychological defense mechanisms. She points to the far right of the defense spectrum she has drawn and explains that denial and projection are the sickest of all defenses. She further explains that anyone who uses this defense is usually some kind of an addict, one who denies they have a problem and projects it into someone else.

Bingo! Could anything better describe what just happened here? It validates my belief that con artists are addicts. In this moment, Cope is silently using the defenses at the far right on the spectrum, the sickest ones—denial and projection.

Coming Face to Face with Dana Cope

Taking a step to the left, I stand in front of Dana Cope. Her once lovely appearance is changed as well; her professionally frosted, long wavy hair has given way to dishwater blonde with several inches of mousy brown roots. She looks homely and heavy. Was this part of the courtroom con as well?

Still I feel sorry for her, believing her to be a fellow victim of her silver-tongued husband. As I prepare to put my arms around her and give her a compassionate hug, I encounter the sensation of attempting to hug a cement post with laser guns focused at my head.

Then I see it. Dana had become sucked into her husband's make-believe world where everything appears upside down and inside out; the guilty are the innocent, and the innocent are the guilty—a world where life is lived more as fiction than as fact. She abetted him and supported him in every way, keeping his books and doing anything else he asked, all the time seeing herself as a loving wife instead of as the enabler she is. How sad to be so duped. In her mind, I'm the bad guy, the one most responsible for getting her husband indicted. Never mind the fact that he more than deserved it and needed to be held accountable.

Enablers are as addicted to protecting the addict as the addict is to, in this case, conning. Enablers never seem to comprehend that by supporting an addict, they're helping destroy them both. They are both denying and projecting. I wish I could make them see that my decision to report Cope did not originate from a personal vendetta. It wasn't my objective to destroy him. My only motivation: To destroy his chances of harming future victims or further harming present victims. I'd heard the victims' stories, and my whole soul ached for them; they had become my friends. I'm certain that Cope is an addict, addicted to image and money, and probably power and control; I realize he can't stop conning unless he is put in prison, where he won't have the chance.

Relieved the encounter appears to be ending, I slowly back away. The huge courtroom doors begin to open. Our case is next. As I move towards the open door, I'm still contemplating this startling picture of a man and his wife I once knew, and I wonder, "How could a religious man allow his mind to bring him to this place, to reduce himself to what he is now?" It's a question many have contemplated.

A quote I once heard came to mind, something to the effect that "Religion at its best is the same as psychotherapy; it's a *movement of the mind* that starts all other movement. Thought puts energy into motion."

As I considered this, my 99% voice whispered, "Any time our confused 1% mind takes hold of anything, it creates problems with that thing. You know that's its nature; it is always confused. Yet, if religion is interpreted by one's 99% mind, it can free and empower an individual.

The voice continued, "You understand that most people don't know they have two minds, or how to get from one to the other; that's why you're writing this book. It's essential information, for if they don't know, they can't control it, and then their fearful 1% mind takes over—it's every person's default setting. This mind uses religion to judge, condemn, separate us from our brother, make us feel less than, and creates guilt. It fosters thoughts that not only separate us from others but also separates us from our divine 99% self. Feeling separated from self, and less than, creates a black hole inside that they attempt to fill with something on the outside. *That's an addiction.*

"With an addiction, enough is never enough because you can't fill up an empty space on the inside with something from the outside, unless what you are attempting to fill is an empty stomach!"

Chapter Three

CON MAN IN THE COURTROOM

*[When we are addicted to instant gratification]...We ignore
[our problems], forget them, and pretend they do not exist,
even take drugs to assist us in ignoring them. We attempt
to get out of them rather than suffer through them.*
—**M. Scott Peck, M.D.**, from *The Road Less Traveled*

During the course of our investigations, I worked closely with an anonymous source who knew Cope well. This person told me that for years, whenever Cope was confronted with his wrongdoing, he would say, "Oh, I'll never get caught and if I do, they'll just put me on probation." That sounded entirely in character. In my last email conversation with Cope, after I told him I was going to the state attorney general, he smugly wrote, *"You can't do a thing to us. We have friends in high places."* The words chilled me then and continued to chill me throughout the investigation.

Reflecting on Cope's words, I realize that when we ignore and pretend, we can only do it for so long and when things finally catch up to us—well, see for yourself.

As those involved in the previous case step out of the courtroom, we file in. The governmental components of our SWAT team sit in the benches at the

29

back left of the room. Dana sits alone in the section to their right. I sit alone in the benches between the two. I must have really stood out, dressed in tangerine, surrounded by empty benches and dark suits.

Finally in the courtroom, I draw a deep breath of warm dry air as strange sensations squiggle around my body. I didn't know whether to interpret them as pain or pleasure; they seemed a hybrid mix.

Cope and his attorney are sitting in front of the wooden rails that divide the audience from the criminals, the attorneys and the judge. I'm sitting behind the rails, behind Cope.

As Judge Anderson wheels himself into the courtroom, we are all asked to stand as the judge lifts himself out of his wheelchair into his chair behind the raised podium.

Those who have been through trauma tend to be more compassionate. Cope plays that like a master violinist plays a Stradivarius. As he approaches the bench, he takes on the posture of deep humility, dropping his head in contrition, answering every question humbly with "Yes, your honor," while drooping his head and keeping his hands crossed over his crotch as if trying to protect his manhood.

What happened next added more frosting to my already stress-frosted hair. Judge Anderson said, "It doesn't look like any of your victims are too upset. None of them are here." In his effort to coddle Cope, I, a victim, have been overlooked as a "nobody." The judge continued to treat Cope as if he were the victim, telling him he didn't have to plead guilty to anything.

Faking the humility stance obviously fooled the judge, but it didn't fool me. Feeling the blood rush to my face, I want to stand up and holler, "Hey, I'm a victim and I'm here! I may not look like one because I'm not in rags, my hair hasn't yet turned completely white, and I'm still alive and sane. (The sane part may be questioned if I said all the things I'd like to say about now.) This is not the case with all the other victims. I know their stories, those that are still alive to tell them.

"Some have lost their sanity and their marriages, to say nothing of their homes and their life savings. How can you expect people who have been so physically and emotionally destroyed to be here? You just don't get it at all, do you? Even if the victims had the money or the emotional energy to get here, which most don't, they don't have the time. Many of them are working three jobs just to keep from losing their homes and put enough food on the table to keep their families from starving. At least one I know is on the verge of a nervous breakdown. And you wonder why Cope's victims aren't here? Ask me and you'll never make that statement again! And perhaps you won't be so solicitous of Cope—he's not the victim here—remember? I know the real victims and Cope's got a place in paradise compared to theirs."

I also wanted to say, again and again, "Hey judge, this is the guy who has conned 100 million bucks from people all over the world. He's a con man, remember? You're supposed to be smart. Don't you get it? He's now conning you."

It was Judge Anderson's job to tell Cope he'd been indicted by a grand jury on thirty-two counts of fraud and money laundering. I believe if it had been up to the judge, he would have let Cope walk out of the courtroom scot-free. When it came time to advise Cope of the indictment, Judge Anderson did so almost apologetically, offering to provide a court-appointed attorney for him at no cost if he couldn't afford one. That seemed a strange statement when he had his high-powered oval-shaped attorney, whom he was paying with money stolen from his "clients," right next to him. Given the man's size, he was difficult to overlook.

Pampering the Criminal

"Sweet" is the best way I can describe Judge Anderson's treatment of Cope—irritatingly sweet. Yes, I guess Cope's subtle conning had gotten to this judge, who had most likely learned compassion from his own pain. But any virtue can become a vice if overdone. His compassion not only seemed overdone—it seemed burnt to a crisp.

Still…why would he go to all that trouble to con the judge? Judge Anderson would not even be the judge who tried the case or determined his sentence. It was the prosecuting attorney who had the most power. He could plea bargain the case and make a recommendation to the judge for a lesser sentence.

Then I realized…it wasn't the judge he was trying to con; it was the U. S. Attorney, David Eisenberg. Eisenberg could accept a plea bargain and let Cope off with a light sentence. That day, Eisenberg was conned into letting Cope off the hook, releasing him on his own recognizance (O/R), meaning no bail and no jail. Apparently, Cope, or someone, had found Eisenberg's vulnerability and played to that as well. There's no logic that would allow Cope, indicted on thirty-two counts, to be out on the streets while his partner, Eddie Bias, found guilty by the grand jury of only one count of conspiracy, sat in jail.

There were some stipulations imposed in conjunction with Cope's being out on O/R, but we soon found they were being violated because we had a private investigator following him. One of the O/R stipulations prohibited him from indulging in any of his former conning "activities." We knew he'd been indulging in them right up until he walked into the courthouse to be officially indicted, but it made no difference. (Later, we'd learn he was violating the conditions of his O/R after his indictment as well. We gave our information to "our guys," an order was drawn up and signed to have him arrested, but it was never executed. He stayed free for years.)

The court proceedings for the indictment didn't last long. The charges were read, Judge Anderson told Cope he didn't have to admit to the charges, and with no word from Cope, considered them denied. Court was adjourned, and the trial set for May 2006. We never got that day in court, because the case was plea-bargained prior to trial. The attorneys would work out a mutually agreeable deal that suited them, not the victims, and we would be asked to participate only in a sentencing hearing to set the punishment.

It is standard court procedure for sentencing to take place no more than ninety days from the time of the plea-bargain. Cope succeeded in postponing his sentencing for over *four* years. Does this sound right to anyone out there? Is our judicial system broken? Or are other factors involved?

Once I returned home from the indictment, I studied my victim's rights and found I had the right to meet with U.S. Attorney Eisenberg. Again I flew back to Phoenix. Another victim, John Anderson, and I met with U.S. Attorney Eisenberg and two members of the SWAT team.

We told Eisenberg of our concerns about letting Cope off too easily, knowing he'd be on the streets conning again. I gave them more information I'd received from another victim in the UK showing Cope had penetrated deeper into the international marketplace. I also shared some of the victim stories I'd collected. For a kicker, I reminded Eisenberg he was going to be famous, for the whole nation would be watching him. A substantial article about the case had recently run in *Forbes* magazine.

A couple of weeks later we find court orders coming from the U. S. Attorney's office…signed by another attorney. It seems that shortly after our meeting with Eisenberg, he and half his staff suddenly quit. Nobody can tell me why, except to say Eisenberg just decided to retire, although it appeared it was right in the prime of his career.

I had a couple of conversations with the new U. S. Attorney, Peter Sexton, who seemed very pleasant. He promised he'd sit down with me after the trial and tell me a lot of things he couldn't tell me at the time. At the sentencing, as you will read, he pushed us through our testimonies, cutting them short, and then rushed out to another case. The promised conversation never took place. I've never heard from him since.

Chapter Four
VICTIMIZED TWICE

*Victims have discovered that they are treated as appendages of a
system appallingly out of balance. They have learned that
somewhere along the way, the system has lost tract of the simple
truth that it is supposed to be fair and to protect those who obey
the law while punishing those who break it. Somewhere along the way, the
system began to serve lawyers and judges and defendants,
treating the victim with institutionalized disinterest.*
— **President Reagan's** Task Force on *Victims of Crime* report,
issued December 1982

This quote describes very accurately what I encountered while pursuing the Cope case. It showed up over and over. It showed up on the day of the indictment, as you just read in the last chapter. It would again show up in giant spades on the day of the sentencing. Victims are tossed aside while the guilty one, Dennis D. Cope, was treated with velvet gloves.

After spending thousands of hours and thousands of dollars helping crack this case, I never expected to be treated as invisible and sometimes worse, as dirt to be swept under a rug.

We'd provided evidence to indicate that Cope had swindled people out of more than one hundred million dollars.

We'd provided information proving Cope's Ponzi schemes had gone international.

We'd provided the IRS with bank account numbers of the scamsters' offshore bank accounts where money was found. We never saw a penny of it, yet Cope was able to access it to pay his high-powered attorneys! How could they allow that? It was *our* money. And what happened to the remainder of that money?

After all we'd done, we deserved better treatment. We deserved better even if we hadn't done anything to help crack the case. We did not get better. Reagan's task force pinpointed the problem in the courts very accurately.

Now the back-story begins. I'll begin by sharing some of emotional stresses I encountered while working to gather needed information for the case.

The Eyes

I had many upsetting experiences during the hunt for Cope. One difficult experience took place under a large tree in a city park south of Provo, Utah, as I sat on a hard metal picnic bench gazing into the sad, vacant, terrified, yet courageous eyes of a group of Cope's victims.

These were my fellow victims whose impact statements we needed for the prosecution in the case against Cope. As each victim related his or her story, my body tensed, my breath came faster, my heart pounded. I cringed as I observed the pain in their eyes, and, being highly sensitive to others' energy, my heart hurt as I picked up their emotional pain. Cope, the con, and Bias, his partner, had destroyed the lives of so many good people. Some had no idea how they'd save their homes, which were mortgaged to the hilt to feed Cope's Ponzi scheme, and others were struggling to put food on the table for their families.

They told their stories, and I took extensive notes in my head. It had been so difficult to coax these victims from the shadows where they attempted to hide from their shame, embarrassment, guilt and fear of the future. It took some time for them to decide they could trust me before they opened up. As they spoke, it was clear the experience was cathartic for them. And I was pleased to now have the stories the prosecution needed to build their case. After everyone had spoken, they left the park, one by one. I sat there all alone for some time. When I tried to unfold my body, intending to walk to my car, my legs would hardly move; I felt as if someone had shoved a giant tube into my energy system and drained away my life force.

My legs felt as if they had been stiffly starched. With great effort, I worked my way to the one lone car left in the parking lot, my little Suzuki Aerio, our budget replacement for the sports car we drove BC (Before Cope). I pulled myself into the car, determined to make the 400-mile drive home, but my entire body felt so heavy and limp it was difficult to maintain a grip on the car's steering wheel. I hadn't gone far when I realized I couldn't drive any farther and pulled into the first motel I could find, and flopped into the sag in the middle of the bed. That's all I remember until morning.

The next morning I reflected on why I'd been so emotionally pained and drained by the stories and realized much of it came from yet unresolved pain that lingered inside from the murders of my mother and sister. It was after that tragedy I resolved to do whatever I could to help victims get their lives back. My resolve was now taking the form of helping Cope victims and trying to prevent him from creating more victims.

The Vampire SWAT Team

In the years leading up to indictment, I worked with a group of professionals from the FBI, the IRS, and various other law enforcement and governmental agencies. I never met most of them; they were emails on the computer screen and voices on the phone. I'd refer to them by their professional affiliation and their first name: "FBI Harold," "CPA Mark." Collectively, I thought of them as the Vampire SWAT Team. I called them our SWAT team, even though they weren't going to use any special weapons in the traditional sense. But I knew we all would have to use special wisdom and tactics in dealing with this slippery duo if we were to be successful. Members of the SWAT team came and went—sometimes in unsettling ways.

IRS Lisa was one of my favorite team members. Her job was to search for money Cope had hidden in foreign bank accounts, and her work was very impressive. Talking to her and others, I got the distinct impression she'd found a lot of money—enough that the state hired a forensic CPA to handle it. (Later the CPA would deny any money ever existed.) Lisa and I seemed to work well together, so when I flew to Phoenix to meet another team member, I decided to call Lisa and ask her to lunch.

I'd expected a warm greeting and a quick invitation to come by her office, so her cold response left me almost speechless.

"No, you can't come by. I'm leaving my job. I'm cleaning out my desk right now." She sounded terrified.

"Where are you going?"

"To work for the Postmaster General." She'd never even mentioned that she was looking for a new job.

Being the persistent person I am, I said, "Oh, I'm on a tight schedule. I'd only stay a minute or two."

"I can't see you." Click.

Lisa was gone, just like that.

It was the last time I ever heard her voice.

That same day, I met Kathleen De La Rosa, our original attorney from the Arizona State Securities Commission. They had the case originally. I met CPA Mark that same day. He worked for the commission as a forensic CPA.

Mark is average looking, tall with dark brown hair, seems intensely interested in figuring me out and quietly absorbs everything that is said. Kathleen appears older and thinner than I expected, and she looks worn out, as if she's carrying a heavy load of tension. I wonder whether the tension comes from her work on the Cope case.

We all indulge in a little social chitchat, and then the questions begin. I answer theirs and they answer mine. I thank them for their efforts and express my feelings about the importance of teamwork in bringing Cope to justice. The State team has worked hard. At that time, Janet Napolitano (now the secretary of Homeland Security) was the Arizona attorney general. She'd put white-collar crime at the top of her priority list, and commission attorneys took these cases seriously.

I felt that if anyone could crack this case, it would be the Arizona women.

Before I left, I had one last question for Kathleen.

"What happened to Lisa? Why is she leaving her position with the IRS?" I asked.

Kathleen dropped her head, shook it from left to right several times, but didn't say a word. I had the impression that Kathleen knew a lot she wanted to reveal but for some reason couldn't. I believe she was trying to tell me with her body language that something had happened and needed to be investigated—but she couldn't say it out loud.

That was the first and last time I ever saw Kathleen.

A few weeks later I called Kathleen's number and an unfamiliar voice answered the phone.

"Could I please speak to Kathleen," I asked politely.

"She's not here anymore," the voice replied.

"Could I speak to Terry, her investigator?" I asked. I'd often worked with Terry when Kathleen wasn't available.

"He's not here anymore," the voice said again.

"Could you tell me where they went," I inquired.

"I don't know."

"Could you put me in touch with someone who does know?"

"No."

I'm determined not to hang up the phone until I get some answers. "Kathleen had been handling a case I started years ago involving Dennis Cope and a Ponzi scheme," I explained. "Who is my contact person now, I continued?"

"Maybe you'd better call the FBI."

"Thank you."

Picking up the phone, I dial the familiar number. FBI Harold answers. I hadn't spoken to him very often; I'd always handled things with Kathleen.

"Harold, I just tried to get in touch with Kathleen and Terry. No one seemed to know what happened to either of them. Can you tell me?"

There's a silence, and when he speaks, it's with lots of pauses and hesitations.

"Umm…a bus hit Kathleen and…um…she was killed."

Harold was new to his job. This was a tough case for a newbie.

I can hardly catch my breath. "Hit by a bus? And killed?"

"Yes…it was an accident."

Seldom am I at a loss for words but now my vocal chords seemed paralyzed. Cope's last words to me, about his friends in high places, forcefully flashed through my mind. I wondered, "Does he *really*?"

Finally, I ask, "Who is going to be my contact person now?"

"Um…I guess I am," Harold says.

In the months that followed, I would become more and more frustrated with Harold. He didn't seem willing to divulge any information.

Later, I looked for more information about Kathleen's death, but no one would answer my questions, and I found no record of it on the Internet. I finally had a research guru look for it. He found the death notice with great difficulty, under her maiden name. The notice was posted quite some time after her death.

When I finally met FBI Harold at the indictment, I was surprised to find a tall, pleasant black man. His winning smile and charming manner reminded me of someone you'd find singing in a church choir or counseling teenagers, rather than being a special agent for the FBI. I liked him immediately in spite of myself.

I also met other members of the SWAT team at the indictment.

IRS Cory, IRS Lisa's Replacement

I'd never clicked with Cory the way I had with Lisa. I know it's unfair, but I have a mild resentment that he's there instead of Lisa. Cory was Harold's opposite: short, Caucasian, and very serious. He seemed cold and distant; he didn't crack even a tiny smile. Perhaps it was because of the weight on his shoulders. He'd had to fill big shoes; maybe he felt my resentment. Perhaps Lisa and I had gotten too close, and he was warned to keep his distance. If so, why?

CPA Mark, Forensic Accountant from the Arizona Corporation Commission

I was delighted to see CPA Mark, and CPA Mark seemed as glad to see me. I got the feeling he sensed the wheels in my mind churning, begging for answers about Kathleen. Before I even asked questions, he told me Kathleen had been riding to work on her moped when she ended up under a bus. She died instantly.

Chills chased each other up and down my body. What was she doing on a moped? How could she just drive under a bus? Cope's veiled threat flashed in my head like a neon sign.

" You can't do anything to us; we have friends in high places!"

I pushed the thought aside for a moment and traded friendly chitchat with the team members. Finally, I decide to try something brazen and see if I can get some answers about this thing that has been bothering me for years about Cope having friends in high places. Does he really, or is this simply a con man maneuver to discourage me from pursuing him?

This was my chance to ask if Cope is protected, although I didn't really expect an answer.

"I know this is a sensitive question, and you may not be able to answer it, but if the answer is yes, just don't say anything. Do you really think Cope has friends in high places?"

For a long time, no one spoke. I began to think I had my answer. Then just as I was becoming confident of it, FBI Harold said, "We don't know." Then the others chimed in, "We don't know."

Mission Accomplished

Despite the strange occurrences, I'd done what I'd set out to do. I'd exposed Cope, tracked down victims and convinced them to tell me their stories. Yet I also assigned myself the task of bird-dogging this case forever if I had to—until we got these Psychic Vampires off the streets. Being a writer and a one-time reporter, I also assigned myself the task of keeping in contact with the media, providing information and compelling stories so the press could inform and protect the public.

We needed the media, because strange things continued to happen; we didn't know whom we could trust, especially because of the pampered treatment Cope got from the prosecuting attorney—no jail, no bail, no consequences for violating his O/R (own recognizance) release. This meant he, indicted on thirty-two criminal counts, was released without bail after promising a judge to appear at future court proceedings. But Cope pushed the privileges. He even got permission to travel out of state where he got involved in another Ponzi scheme. Do all those special privileges sound strange to anyone but me?

Even after the indictment, the victims' needs were largely ignored until I wrote a few indignant letters to the judge and to the assistant U.S. attorney who was prosecuting the case, expressing our concerns about being re-victimized. That's when the prosecuting attorney called and said we would talk after the sentencing, but, as I said before, that never happened.

Now that you've had a sneak preview of the courtroom scene in which Cope was officially indicted, we'll begin the part of the back-story that reveals how and why we got sucked into the Ponzi scheme—and ended up in the federal courts.

Chapter Five

FEAR MAKES US VULNERABLE

*If you want to enslave people without physical force, you have
to feed the population with a little fear so they will be vulnerable.*
— **Hans Peter Duerr**, nuclear physicist

It took me a long time to realize it, but the fact is, I was vulnerable to Cope's scam because I harbored unconscious fears without even being aware of them. That's true of all the other victims as well. Some of these early fears were closer to the surface, such as, "I'm not enough on my own. I must have more money to mean anything." Other fears were buried deep in the unconscious and were not so readily available. Any kind of fear makes us vulnerable. *Good con men can sense vulnerability as surely as a predator senses its prey. That's what makes them so deadly.*

Living in our 1% world, being unaware of what is real, makes us vulnerable to attacks from psychic vampires. These are people who drain the energy and life force from others, becoming stronger as their victims become weaker. . Psychologist Joe Slate wrote about the destructive force of these beings in his book, *Psychic Vampires.* As long as we have psychic wounds, even if we're not aware of them, there will always be psychic vampires ready to feed on them. I was one of the unaware.

The main psychic vampire in this drama is named Dennis D. Cope.

Psychic Wounds Attract Psychic Vampires

In the spring of 2000, I was living in Phoenix, newly married to Bob. It was a second marriage for me, the fifth for him. We'd already raised families (eight kids for me, four for him!), and we were both retired and enjoying each other's company. Between our retirement income and my savings, we could afford a nice, comfortable lifestyle.

A friend of Bob's urged him to get together with Dennis Cope's friend who explained that Cope was a high-powered investment advisor with a fabulous business deal, one that promised a high rate of return. But before Cope would let us in on this amazing opportunity, we had to meet with one of his lesser colleagues before we could meet with the god source himself.

We met the accountant for breakfast. He told us about some of the ways the Cope organization was making money. The stories changed so fast over time I don't remember exactly what he was promoting, except the 10% per month return.

Being in business myself, I asked the accountant some very pointed questions. Looking back, I can see how that made him defensive; he couldn't answer the questions well. That was the first red flag I missed. My hidden psychic wounds and vulnerabilities made me vulnerable to an enticing scam.

Con artists are only one manifestation of psychic vampires. We all have these creatures in our lives. Living in this world of fear and confusion, we can't avoid them. Even well-meaning parents and teachers create the wounds that attract and nourish them.

Psychic Wounds—A By-Product of Living in a 1% World

We often get things backwards when we're raising our kids and, with the best of intentions, create psychic wounds. Here's a simple example. Johnny runs up the walk, falls, skins his knee and begins to cry. His parent, trying to make Johnny tough, says something like, "Big boys don't cry. You're not really hurt." But the child's knee does hurt and he feels like crying. What the parent has unknowingly done is tell the child he can't trust his own feelings. Many of the people involved in this Ponzi scheme fell into that category of not trusting their own feelings and instincts.

Once you're aware of it, this kind of messaging is everywhere. Advertisements rely on creating psychic wounds, exploiting feelings of insecurity about our looks, our popularity, and status. The companies have to make us wrong to sell us something to make us right.

What about the schools? Well, think of how often our mistakes were pointed out, in red ink, and how rarely our strengths were noticed.

George H. Reavis was Assistant Superintendent of Schools in Cincinnati, Ohio, over a half-century ago. In the 1940s, he wrote *The Animal School,* and over the years, variations keep surfacing, for the fable cleverly points out the flaws of education, which are still relevant today.

The Animal School

Once upon a time, the animals decided they must do something heroic to meet the problems of "a new world." So they organized a school.

They adopted an activity curriculum consisting of running, climbing, swimming, and flying. To make it easier to administer the curriculum all the animals took all the subjects.

The duck was excellent in swimming, better than his instructor, in fact, but he made only passing grades in flying and was very poor in running. Since he needed to improve in running, he had to stay after school and also drop swimming in order to practice running. This was kept up until his web feet were badly worn, and he was only average in swimming. But average was acceptable in school, so nobody worried about that, except the duck.

The rabbit started at the top of the class in running but had a nervous breakdown because of so much make-up work in swimming.

The squirrel was excellent in climbing until he developed frustration in the flying class where his teacher made him start from the ground up instead of from the tree top down. He also developed a charlie horse from overexertion and then got a C in climbing and a D in running.

The eagle was a problem child and was disciplined severely. In the climbing class, he beat all the others to the top of the tree but insisted on using his own way to get there.

At the end of the year, an abnormal eel that could swim exceedingly well, and also run, climb, and fly a little, had the highest average and was valedictorian.

Dr. Reavis understood how schools make the student feel "not okay."

What about religions? While they began as a way to *reconnect* us with our creator, the ego mind has stepped in and taken over in many cases. According to Dr. David Hawkins, a psychiatrist who wrote *Power vs. Force,* formal religion's constant emphasis that man is a sinner fills us with fear, guilt and shame; these are the very thoughts and emotions that *separate* us from our creator and disempower us.

This is not about blaming those who raise us and educate us, or those who are just trying to make a living. It's merely to point out that psychic wounds are inevitable; it's a consequence of living in this confused world of chaos and 1% thinking.

In the wake of my terrible experience with Cope, I began examining myself to find my own wounds that had made me vulnerable to being conned.

How I Missed the First Red Flag

After sparring with the accountant, I blamed myself. "I'm too aggressive," I thought. "I threaten men, I should have handled things differently."

I grew up in an environment with significant people in my life who found fault with everyone; it bothered me terribly. I didn't want to be that way, and I decided I'd always look for the good in people and never find fault. Bingo! A vulnerability was born. I couldn't see the fault, the red flag, because I'd programmed myself not to.

Then I realized I had become like those I resented. While I didn't find fault with others, I was constantly finding fault with myself, as in blaming myself for being too aggressive. Bingo! I'd created another vulnerability. By constantly criticizing myself, I'd stopped trusting my instincts. There were two psychic wounds right there. I was a perfect candidate for a psychic vampire.

These wounds leave us feeling like we're not enough. We don't feel smart enough, pretty enough, or rich enough—and money will fix everything. It will buy a good education, a new face, and a new car—almost anything. It's the perfect hook for con men to pull in their prey. It's especially good for those who correlate their self worth with their net worth.

This is why people smart enough to make millions of dollars can be dumb enough to give it away to a con man. Actually, it has nothing to do with smart or dumb; it has everything to do with our vulnerabilities. If you're interested in more details on who's most vulnerable to being conned, go to the website www. RisingFromAshes.net to obtain the *Special Report: Are You the Next Victim of a Con Man?*

The awareness of what is now in the special report came much later, long after Cope had done his damage.

Chapter Six

HOW CON MEN
MANIPULATE OUR PERCEPTIONS

...We never really experience the universe directly, we just experience...
our perception of it...our only universe is perception.
—**Alan Moore**, visionary author of *Watchmen*

Cope was able to enter my universe and wreck it because he knew how to manipulate my perceptions. We can defend ourselves against con men when we realize that our psychic wounds make it easy for a skilled cheat to distort our view of the world.

Meeting Cope and Missing the Second Red Flag

After the initial meeting with Cope's accountant friend, I first met Dennis D. Cope himself in Laughlin, Nevada, at a gambling casino. Cope had already formed an investment group for us to join—the Millennium Group—and we had gathered to see Cope and hear more details about this business opportunity. Excitement stirred the air. So many of the good-hearted, capable people my husband and I met that night seemed to think of Cope almost as a demi-God. I didn't know it then but we were all about to get an up close and personal experience of how con artists can make us see white when we're looking at black.

Suddenly, "Cope the Great" appeared with his sidekick, Dan, a loyal devotee who looked sweet, naïve and as innocent as a newborn baby. He was a good foil for Cope. Dressed in his Armani-looking suit, with his good looks, nice build and $10,000 smile, Cope looked like he'd just stepped out of *GQ* magazine. But despite the slick appearance, I was a little underwhelmed by Cope—until he began to speak.

He was a natural orator. There was a hypnotic quality to his voice, casting a spell on his audience, mesmerizing us into believing anything he said.

Cope (far right) later attached himself to another
Ponzi schemer, Eddie Bias (far left).

To further their scams, ones they ran together and individually, Cope and Bias bought a bogus bank and sent out worthless certificates of deposit (shown above).

A Riverboat Gambler

In the aftermath of my involvement with Cope, some people have asked if I had any doubts about Cope during that first encounter.

The answer to that is…yes and no. My 99% self had plenty of doubts and tried to warn me that he wasn't credible. As he started to speak, a movie played behind my eyes. It featured a mustachioed riverboat gambler with the face of Cope. He was slipping a card up his sleeve.

However, my 1% voice, the one generated by my 1% mind, quickly silenced my intuition. I even chastised myself for those thoughts. I didn't want them. I didn't want to find fault with Cope. I wanted to see him as the business guru everyone believed him to be, with all the powers he claimed so he could make us all rich. I must have gotten the wrong impression, I told myself.

Another clue missed because of my vulnerability.

A similar incident occurred with another victim, Michelle. As her husband Robert began to present the "opportunity" to invest with Cope, she also had a movie behind her eyes. A big blanket dropped in front of her, shutting her off from her husband, warning her about what he was proposing. Yet she trusted him more than her inner voice, and they gave Cope over a half million dollars. Our husbands had mutual strengths/vulnerabilities. Both were risk-takers, retired fighter pilots.

Legitimate doubts are easy to overcome when you don't want them. After we turned over our money to Cope, we were even more reluctant to doubt him. That meant we'd have to face the fact that he was a fraud and we'd lost all our money. Even after Cope was indicted, there were those who still believed he was going to return their money with all the promised interest, because they couldn't stand to face the shocking truth.

It is much easier to believe a lie than it is to see the truth if you'd rather believe the lie. We don't see things as they are; we see things as we are. That is what makes us so vulnerable to con men—our unmet needs. These unmet needs become our psychic wounds; our psychic wounds become our vulnerabilities. Our vulnerabilities make us want to see the lie.

As the meeting went on, Cope continued to mesmerize his audience. By the time he walked out of the room, we were convinced he was a genius, a high-flying financier—someone beyond questioning. We felt privileged to even walk by him and his gorgeous wife and say, "Hello."

One of the things that impressed us most was Cope's history as a seminary teacher for the youth of his church—a church shared by many in the audience. Generally these men are picked for their moral strength and their ability to influence. They got the influence part right! Later I found out he didn't go through the screening process to become a credentialed, paid teacher. Instead, he was simply an untrained volunteer. But we didn't know that then, and Cope's claim of being a seminary teacher gave him great credibility.

Manipulating Us Through Our Strengths

People like Cope can exploit our strengths, as well as our weaknesses. Many, perhaps most, of his victims loved the church they shared and all it represented; this is generally considered a strength. He exploited that strength and crafted words to manipulate us. To those in the group who belonged to his church, the millennium was a time when Christ would come and reign for a thousand years, bringing peace and prosperity. He didn't miss a trick. He named our group the Millennium Group.

Yet all of his meetings were held in gambling casinos. Strange for a religious man who didn't believe in gambling—another clue I missed. Cope was a walking, talking contradiction.

At the next meeting—at the Golden Nugget Casino in Las Vegas—something startling happened. I walked in late for the meeting because I couldn't get an early enough flight. Cope was in the middle of his compelling speech as I arrived, just in time to see one bright, courageous young man, less vulnerable than the rest, stand up. Mincing no words, he asked, "Are you legitimate, or is this a scam?"

I froze, as did the rest of those in the room.

We all held our breath as we waited for Cope to respond. I could see intense anger welling up inside him, as if he was offended that this impudent young man would dare to question him.

I thought Cope was going to blow, but pacing back and forth across the stage helped him contain his rage. Finally, he just glared at the young man and asked in crisp measured tones, "Do – you – want – your – money – back?

His body language, his voice—it all implied, "You idiot! You're stupid to question me, and you're the stupidest person on the planet if you get out now!" It shut up that young man, along with the rest of us who might have had the audacity to ask a question. I never saw the young man again, and I wonder if he ever got his money back.

I'd seen this "quieting" tactic used before. During another meeting, with Cope's cohort Dan, an astute businesswoman, Sandra, asked Dan for clarification on some of the points he'd just made, explaining she didn't understand. Dan said indignantly, "Well, everyone else does!"

That dismissal, implying that the lack of understanding was *her* fault, kept her quiet. It had the same effect on everyone in the room and kept them from asking questions. As I write now, it stuns me to think we invested anyway. But then with my mind firmly enmeshed in 1% thinking, I was an easy target.

Investing Anyway

Cope promised us returns of 10 percent a month on our investment. My husband, Bob, and I talked it over and went ahead with it. We reasoned that even if we didn't get the returns promised, our original investment was safe; after all, we were told our money would never leave the bank. A Wells Fargo employee at the bank where Cope told us to deposit our money confirmed this promise that our money would never leave the bank. We later learned that Cope had allegedly bribed this bank official up to $20,000 a week to tell us that, when he knew our money was going straight into Cope's bank account.

In the lawsuit against Wells Fargo, a letter was presented, signed by a bank official from this branch, assuring us our money would never leave the bank. The judge would not allow it into evidence. The prosecutor showed up in court with a burned face and bloodshot eyes and completely blew the case. Was there bribery involved? We can't prove it.

But all this evidence came later. At the time we "invested," we had no idea Cope might have bribed a bank official. We truly believed our money was safe in the bank, even if we didn't make the promised 10 percent a month.

More Vulnerabilities

Through examining these events, I've realized that most of my vulnerabilities revolved around family wounds and family traumas, both old and new. It was much the same for the other victims I spoke to.

What were my vulnerabilities?

First, I was in a new marriage and very much wanted it to work. Bing! A big vulnerability! A good friend introduced my husband to this "business opportunity." We were doing fine on our retirement income, but Bob really wanted to invest with Cope. He had no money, but I did, and I think that bothered him. The "investment" was a combination of his idea and my money. It was a project we could take on together.

Second, I still carried psychic wounds over the failure of my first marriage. I stayed in it much longer than was wise, and then I had a direct revelation that I would die if I didn't leave. I doubted my husband would do me physical harm. But living in a box where someone else controls your mind does cause psychological damage; if it's severe enough and goes on long enough, it can cause death. With a decreased will to live, we can unconsciously create an accident, a heart attack, or cancer. I'd already tried cancer. But no matter how much that marriage needed to end, in my culture divorce was highly frowned upon. I just couldn't face it, especially with eight children. I could hardly say the D word without feeling I was swearing. But after this revelation I had no choice.

Without meaning to, my ex-husband and I both made the divorce much more difficult than it needed to be, and that was hard on our children. Seven years later, three months after I'd remarried, my first husband died. His death exacerbated my guilt. Bing! Another psychic wound emerged. "Now I *do* need more money," I thought. "If I could make the money Cope promised, I could give each of my children a hundred grand and maybe that would soothe the pain of their dad's death and ease my guilt."

Of course, I know now that giving them the money would have been a huge mistake. It would only have exacerbated our mutual 1% mindset that money solves all problems—but that's where I was then. I had my feet firmly planted in my 1% world of thought.

The vulnerabilities didn't end there. The granddaddy of psychic wounds, which produced as much guilt as the rest of them put together, had its roots in a devastating incident that occurred years before.

It was not long before my first husband and I divorced that my mother and sister were brutally murdered. My niece witnessed the horror but wasn't killed. Observing her in the years since, I sensed she had a huge case of survivor guilt because she kept unconsciously sabotaging her life and her happiness. Guilt always demands punishment.

What I didn't understand was *I was doing the same thing.* It took years more to realize I had survivor guilt too, and I'd been sabotaging my life ever since the murders happened. I'd created many of the traumas in my life my niece had. I gave tens of thousands of dollars to people I barely knew; I moved from a 10,000-square-foot house to renting a bedroom in someone else's house; I blew the last of my life's savings in a Ponzi scheme. All because I was living in the chaos and confusion produced by my 1% thinking—feeling guilty and punishing myself, perhaps thinking I'd take care of my own punishment before the big guy upstairs with the huge punishing tools got hold of me.

My guilt stemmed from two incidents.

First, the day of the murders I saw one of the killers on the road near the cabin where my mother and sister were murdered. I knew he didn't belong there, and I had a premonition he was going to rob someone—but I didn't call the police. I knew the police want to be called when something suspicious happens, so they can prevent a looming crime. I knew that well, having organized one of the first neighborhood watch programs in the country. The police had been at my house and given a lecture to our Neighborhood Watch group on that very topic. I should have called the police. The killers did rob other cabins. That's where they got the guns they used to kill my mother and sister and shoot my brother-in-law.

Second, I left the cabin when my sister wanted me to stay. Looking back, I believe she had a premonition of danger and wanted the comfort of family around her. When I left, she got our mother to stay with her. Our mother was killed with her—instead of me.

Add up all those vulnerabilities, and I was a poster child-perfect target for a con man. But one doesn't have to have the deep and dramatic psychic wounds I had to produce enough guilt to begin sabotaging one's life. Any kind of guilt will do. We all have guilt programmed into our subconscious to some degree. Guilt stems from judgment. We have been programmed to be judgmental of others and ourselves as others have been programmed to judge us. It's all a part of our default ego thinking, our 1% mind at work.

Though I had my vulnerabilities, I was still a warrior. I'd go for the jugular of anyone I saw victimizing others to get gain for themselves. Perhaps it was a way of making restitution for not being able to protect my mother and sister. Whatever the case, Cope underestimated his victims, especially me! I was just a lone woman, a weaker member of the human race, according to his belief system—a belief system that didn't see women as strong enough to take on the role I embraced.

Chapter Seven

HOW WE FOUGHT BACK

All it takes for evil to flourish is for good men [and women] to do nothing.
—**Edmund Burke**, 18th century Irish statesman

Claudia Nelson is the best gumshoe vigilante I have ever met.
She is that rare investor who fought back with the same cunning
and guile as the con men who victimized her. Others would have
walked away—not Nelson. Her 8-year odyssey to bring a
master con artist to justice is inspiring and ultimately satisfying.
Along the way she corrals fellow fraud victims, the FBI,
the Justice Department and the IRS to see the case through.
— **Dirk Smillie**, *Forbes* magazine senior writer

Cope thought our power was in our money and he had it all—therefore we'd be harmless. Was he ever mistaken! He had taken our money, but he hadn't robbed us of our ingenuity or our persistence, or our 99% minds which again began to speak up—and this time we listened.

Cope's inner circle began to lose their unity, and the schemes slowly began to come apart. We knew they were the vulnerable ones now. We made our move and loosely organized ourselves. As we began to warn people who might approach Cope's "event horizon" (the closest you can get to a black hole before being sucked in and crushed), we began to curtail his ability to suck more people into his "black hole." More and more people began asking for their money back. He'd always promised he'd return the principal to anyone who asked, but he never did.

A Ponzi scheme can only work as long as the scammers are bringing in more money than they're giving out. Our efforts slowed their inflow of cash and hastened the collapse of the whole enterprise.

Fighting Cope's Darkness

While Cope and Company were spinning webs to ensnare their next victims, unknown to them, we, the victims, were spinning our own.

The first step was getting Cope to reveal himself. Then we could get him into prison to make certain he couldn't create any more black holes for any more victims. It took me a year to get the info I needed, but I did it. Every time one strategy failed, I'd try another. My philosophy is summed up in this wall-hanging in my office:

NEVER GIVE UP!

I began by sending polite but persistent emails asking about our investment; I sent light-hearted and humorous emails; I invited him out to dinner; I offered to work at his office to clear up whatever organizational problem was keeping us from getting our money; I tried to organize a meditation and prayer group to get this thing out of neutral and over the top. Nothing worked.

Finally, I decided I'd go to the attorney general's office to get the investors some help. I told Cope. He cleverly reminded me that he was one of the biggest investors, so he had more at stake than most of us. He asked me to give him six months to solve things, and if he couldn't resolve the problems, he would go with me to the AG's office. Duh!

I waited another six months. When it came time to make the appointment, Cope said he'd be out of town and asked me to wait until he got back. Would that have been the next week, the next year or the next decade, if at all?

I'd finally had enough. I said, "No way! I'm going without you. You can make your own appointment." That's when he uttered the words that haunted me for the remainder of the case. They'd play in my head every time someone on the case disappeared, every time he got another postponement of sentencing, every time the officials and the court system did nothing to him. The words:

"You can't do a thing to us. We have friends in high places."

I couldn't let Cope have the last nasty word trying to disempower us. And I knew the top six statewide positions in Arizona were occupied by women who worked together and supported each other. I challenged him and said, *"Just watch what a group of women can do when they get together." The moment I recovered from the shock that I'd been conned, I made up my mind...I was going after him!*

Arizona, Here I Come

...right back where I started from.

Cope lived in Arizona. We lived in Arizona when we learned of him, then moved to Idaho. It was from our new home in Boise that we invested my life savings. After all this time, I was as reluctant as anyone to admit I'd been conned, but I could no longer deny it. It was time to stop talking—and take action!

I made a reservation to fly to Phoenix that very day I admitted to myself that I'd been conned. Tickets to Phoenix are not in great demand in July's 120-degree weather, so I had no trouble securing a seat. Less than an hour after takeoff, we stopped in Salt Lake City. I grabbed my cell phone and called the attorney general's office in Phoenix to let them know I was on my way and expected to see the attorney general herself. And I told them why.

The low-level clerk began to stammer and explain that it's impossible to see her without a prior appointment, and without filling out a pile of forms, etc., etc., etc. I told the clerk: "I'm on my way, and I'm going to be in your office in about two hours with my suitcase in tow. I'm not leaving until I get some satisfaction."

"You want I get someone to break his legs?"

After deplaning in Phoenix, I walked through the airport and outside into the suffocating July heat, where I grabbed a cab.

"Take me to the attorney general's office," I instructed the cabbie.

The destination piqued the curiosity of the cabdriver, who asked, "Why are you going there?"

Startled by his intrusion into my private affairs, I hesitated to respond. Then I realized I'd never see him again and decided to use his question as an opportunity to unload the pain I carried from all the devastating stories I'd collected from Cope's victims.

He listened intently to my story, and then asked, *"You want I get someone to break his legs?"*

My heart started to pound. I felt like I'd stepped right into the middle of a Mafia movie but what startled me even more was my reaction to his offer. I was shocked when I realized I was actually contemplating taking him up on that offer!

By now, the cabdriver was as angry at Cope as I was and he tried hard to convince me to accept his offer. I knew I'd better get out before I weakened. I offered a fake smile, pressed a bill into his hand, stepped out of the cab, and started up the stairs with my rolling suitcase bumping behind me, wondering if the cabbie was part of the same Mafia family that Bias had conned, wondering if that is why he seemed to have a deep personal interest in my story. Checking my watch, I saw that exactly two hours had passed since I made the call from the Salt Lake City airport to this office.

I pushed through the door to face a rack full of brochures and forms on my right. To my left, behind what I assume to be a bulletproof window was the receptionist. I announced my arrival, but that was unnecessary. My suitcase was my calling card.

They wasted no time asking me to fill out forms. My demeanor told them I was a woman on a mission and unless they wanted to be mowed down, they'd best not get in my way. They'd already made an appointment for me with the attorney general's lawyers at the Corporation Commission across the street.

At the attorney's offices, Wendy, a pleasant slightly overweight red-headed woman in her late thirties to mid-forties, greets me. When I told my story to her and her investigator, she came close to being shocked. At first, I thought it was because of how horrible the fraud was, and I was glad to have her on our side. (I later found out she knew Cope socially. She wisely withdrew herself from the case.)

This was the beginning of the process—but I had no idea how long the process would take. And I didn't know that Cope would leave another boatload of destruction in his wake before we finally got him in prison.

After the Indictment

That's a nutshell version of how I went from "investing" with Cope to investigating him. From the summer of 2000 to the summer of 2001, I worked to flush out Cope and his illegal activities. From 2001 to 2005, I concentrated on gathering information for the courts to make certain he was put away for a long time, until he was too old to create more victims.

Just as Woodward and Bernstein had developed a "Deep Throat" who fed them information on Watergate, I too developed a credible source who fed me valuable information. I worked with my "Deep Throat" to accumulate information and evidence to present to the FBI and the courts, searching out victims to get their stories for trial, writing letters to the judge when Cope violated the terms of his O/R after his indictment, and questioning why they did nothing to him. We had resources to check what was going on in the courts.

It took a lot of time to track down victims and interview them for stories we could present to the jury. Then, with my limited resources of time and money, I tried to help them any way I could. They often were difficult to work with; they were still traumatized and reluctant to come forth. We needed their stories for the jury, anticipating that the case would go to trial.

By 2006, my inside source had pretty much disappeared. On my own, I continued, and still continue, to connect with the victims and the media, to get information to the public to protect them from con men. Recently, the public television investment show *MoneyTrack* broadcast a feature on the Cope case in their "Scam Alert" series. You can find a link to the segment at the *MoneyTrack* site, www.moneytrack.org, or at my website, www.RisingFromAshes.net, under "Media" information.

One turning point came on September 19, 2005, when *Forbes* magazine published a wonderful article, which helped our cause immensely and led to more media exposure.

It began when Dirk Smillie, a senior writer with *Forbes*, was searching the Internet for material for a new fraud article and picked up the Cope story from an article in the *Arizona Republic*. My name was mentioned in the article, and he did some extensive detective work to locate me. When he found me, I was as excited as he was because I knew silence is a con man's best friend and exposure, his worst enemy. I was delighted to cooperate with Dirk and do anything I could to help expose Cope, the con, and his buddy, Eddie Bias, and forewarn and protect the public.

After about four interviews, asking me many of the same questions over and over until he was satisfied I was credible, Dirk began to trust me as a reliable source. His instincts were accurate; I had gathered more reliable information about the case than any other person. Thanks to the Internet, other people who had been burned by Cope from other countries, and in other groups, read about our investigation and sent me information. I followed up with personal meetings when I could, and these people cautiously revealed their stories. I shared these stories with Dirk for his article.

The Avengers

When authorities shrugged at a $100 million investment scam, angry backers turned into gumshoe vigilantes | By Dirk Smillie

Growing doubts: Investor Claudio Nelson

Other victims pitched in, of course. Because Cope's group was losing their unity, they left a crack in the door and we shoved our foot in and pushed. We informally organized ourselves to divide the work and cover all the bases to keep Cope from escaping justice or harming others. While we waited for Cope's sentencing, Robert B., one member of the group, contacted John Walsh of *America's Most Wanted*, who promised to run the story if Cope tried to escape the country.

Another member, Roger C., discovered the church Cope was going to in South Dakota and warned the head of that congregation that Cope was coming and to beware. Roger's wife went to South Dakota to take pictures of Cope's convenience store; he claimed he shouldn't be sent to prison because he had to run the store. The "store" ended up being a little room with a few tattered magazines and a table, instead of a fully stocked store. We turned that information into the FBI. But then, almost as if someone had warned him he needed a real store, he had one. He called it "Cope With It."

The Universe continued to provide us with information, which I continued to turn over to the FBI and the courts. Then in 2008, Dirk Smillie called and asked if I knew a Dusty Cope. He'd found out that Dusty was connected with a Ponzi scheme in California.

I knew him all right. Dusty was Denny's son, and Denny had gotten involved with, or initiated, Dusty's scam…while he was still under indictment for our Millennium Group scheme. When I called the prosecuting attorney and told him Cope was probably involved in another Ponzi scheme, he said he already knew about it. Yet Cope still was not in jail! I confronted him with the impropriety of Cope still being out on his O/R, and he knew he had to finally put him into jail.

As you can see I kept pretty busy trying to make certain this case didn't fall through some Cope-created crack, and that Cope and Bias were put in prison so they couldn't create more victims. The experience was exhausting and frustrating, and I would find in the end that fighting fraud with war against the perpetrators was a 1% solution to a 1% problem. I was trying to solve the problem at the same level of thinking I was at when I created it. But what else do you know if you are living a confused, chaotic, 1% life? Had I been living fully in my 99% world, I'd have never become a victim of the Ponzi scheme in the first place.

Chapter Eight

CON MEN ARE PSYCHIC VAMPIRES...
WHO LIVE OFF PSYCHIC WOUNDS

A psychic vampire is "Anyone who lives by preying on others."
—**Dr. Joe Slate**, author of *Psychic Vampires*

In this chapter you'll come to understand some small part of the destruction Cope left in his wake. You'll also see that his kind have been around for a very long time. The Biblical story of Cain killing his brother Abel to enrich himself is an early recorded psychic vampire attack, and psychic vampires have been breeding, reproducing and attacking ever since. Their agenda remains the same: to empower themselves, even if it means disempowering others.

Understanding Vampire Myth and Folklore

For centuries, humans have told and retold stories about dead bodies that come to life at night and use their dagger-like fangs to suck the blood of sleeping victims. We call them vampires. We know vampires aren't real but still the stories persist. To understand why and how psychic vampires come about, we need to understand a bit about myth and folklore.

The works of Joseph Campbell and other mythologists help us understand that myths—once primarily read for entertainment—hold great lessons.

Looking beneath the surface and understanding the symbolism, myths contain great wisdom passed on by the ancient ones who lacked the sophistication to express this intuitive wisdom with real understanding. Thus myths and folklore were born.

As our society has become more educated, we now study myths and folklore with much more clarity. As educators and academics analyze vampire mythology from a more sophisticated perspective, they gain deeper insights into human nature. Psychologists today study the concept of vampirism to discover deeper symbolic meaning.

One major study began with psychologist Joe Slate. He found that vampires do exist, but not quite as the mythmakers describe them. Dr. Slate has redefined the old mythological vampires as psychic vampires. They are very real.

What Is a Psychic Vampire?

Dr. Joe Slate began his interest in psychic vampirism when he received a research contract to study the human energy system from a seemingly unlikely source—the U.S. army missile Research and Development Command. He was charged with the responsibility of investigating the energy field enveloping the human body.

In his book *Psychic Vampires,* Dr. Slate said, "It became increasingly evident that this external energy system, commonly called the human aura, was but an outward manifestation of a dynamic internal energy system...that is affected by the mental and physical state of the individual..." After all his research, he expanded the concept of psychic vampires. He now describes psychic vampires as "anyone who lives by preying on others." A con man who sucks all the financial life from his victims is one kind of psychic vampire, the kind I, along with so many others, became a victim of.

Shorted Wiring, Damaged Auras

For centuries, Eastern mystics and healers have been aware that an electrical energy vibrates in and around the human body, commonly called the aura. Auras are visible as color by very intuitive and sensitive individuals; some believe the halo often depicted around Jesus' head is one example of a visible aura. Practitioners of alternative medicine also believe that one's aura reveals the state of one's emotional health. Dr. Slate explains that psychic vampire attacks show up as black holes in a person's aura.

Kirlian cameras enable us to photograph auras and detect this emotional damage. While some physicians still practicing traditional Western medicine question this method, more and more medical professionals are opening up to and recognizing what Eastern mystics and healers have recognized for generations: We do have an emotional energy field that surrounds us and reveals our emotional state of mind. Even the U.S. government acknowledged it when they hired Dr. Slate to study it.

Being the researcher I am, I had to try it. I had my aura photographed twice, first when under a great deal of stress as the result of a series of psychic vampire attacks. (See Image One.) Here it is in black and white; the color photos can be found on the RisingFromAshes.Net website under— Aura Photos. You'll notice the machine picked up very little color; it is mostly darkness that surrounds me. There are so many black holes, they all run together, leaving an almost solid sheet of black encompassing me.

Image One   Image Two

Now look at Image Two. The aura is bright and symmetrical, with a good color. This photo was taken after I had begun to heal myself, using techniques I share in Section Three.

It's important to pay attention to the state of our emotional energy system, just as it's important to fix flawed wiring in a house. A house with a damaged electrical system can have problems as minor as an electrical outlet that won't work, or a house full of lights that won't turn on. If the damage is serious enough, wires setting off sparks, can cause the whole structure to burn down.

Such is the fate of the victims of psychic vampires. A minor attack may prevent one small body part from functioning optimally because it is not receiving the energy it needs. Severe and/or repeated attacks can cause major damage. If the electrical damage has been prolonged and intense, a major organ can burn out. If several organs are affected severely enough, one could die.

Knowing all this, how could I not do something to stop Cope, especially when I knew he'd gone international and my research showed the devastation these Ponzi schemes had done worldwide?

The Original Ponzi

By the summer of 2004, we were well into our legal pursuit of Cope. I started studying up on crime and corruption, becoming educated on the hideous role Ponzi schemes have played through history around the world.

The scheme by that name has been around for almost a century. In 1920 Charles Ponzi conned $9.8 million from victims in Boston (including three-quarters of the police force). Ponzi enticed his victims by offering profits of 50 percent every 45 days. He collected $9.8 million, returned $7.8 million to investors, and then pocketed more than $2 million—an enormous sum of money in 1920 for eight months' work. After being sent to prison for too short a term, he was released and began conning again, this time selling land covered by water. Charles Ponzi provides evidence that con men are addicts and can't stop their compulsive need to con.

Today, Ponzi schemes thrive on the international scene as well, especially in economically deprived countries. Residents of these countries often are desperate; they are vulnerable and become easy prey for these schemes. Albania and the Philippines are two countries that were nearly destroyed by Ponzi schemes.

After my experience and research, I could easily see how people are sucked into the Ponzi scheme. They seem so credible. We check references and see that people actually were paid the high interest promised, only to learn later that the first group of investors was paid with the money from the second group of investors. The first group becomes the credibility for would-be investors doing their due diligence before investing. In effect, those in the first group unknowingly serve as pawns in the Ponzi scheme.

It's easy to understand why most of these schemes go unreported. People feel stupid; they're too embarrassed to go to the authorities, or may have no money to hire an attorney. For those who do, it may cost more to prosecute than what they lost. Consequently, over 90% of those conned never report the crime.

As I read all the research I've compiled, I more clearly understand why I spent my few remaining resources to support what Dirk Smillie called my "gumshoe vigilante efforts." It goes far beyond my refusal to be victimized any longer. Someone has to stand up and say, "Enough is enough," expose these deadly vampires and stop, or at least slow down, their diabolical efforts and protect future victims. I'd also continue to do all I could to help present victims. I'm driven by a quote from Edmund Burke, which I used earlier in the book: *All it takes for evil to flourish is for good men [and women] to do nothing.*

I'm determined to make all the noise I can to protect future victims from these psychic vampires. I'm shouting to the world: Be aware of psychic vampires who live in the shadows and attack the naive and vulnerable for...all of us are naive and vulnerable at some time. And remember...as long as there are psychic wounds, there will always be psychic vampires to feed on them

Then my thoughts turn to Cope. Why would he turn to the dark side? Maybe someone abused him as a child. Usually, those who have been abused abuse others. Maybe he needs help rather than punishment.

Then I remember an episode of the television show *Criminal Minds.*

A detective is interviewing a sadistic killer in an interrogation room. The detective scoots his wooden chair across the floor until his knees nearly touch those of the killer. He looks him straight in the eyes and says, "Your old man beat you, didn't he? He beat you over and over and over again. And your mother didn't protect you, did she? And why didn't she protect you? Because he beat her too, didn't he?"

The criminal turns his head to break eye contact with the interrogator. "Leave my mother out of this," he snarls, and then slowly twists his head back with short deliberate motions. He looks the interrogator square in the eyes, studies him for a few moments and with psychic precision, tunes into the interrogator's own childhood, and says, "You and I are not so different."

The interrogator remains silent for a few moments, stands up to walk off, then turns around, and again looks the killer straight in the eye. "Some who have been abused continue to abuse. Others choose to become cops and try to find the abusers and stop them from abusing others. There's choice here."

As I begin to process that image, my internal conflict weakens. I draw myself back into the present; I'm thinking whatever Cope's reasons for becoming a criminal, abuse or otherwise, he made the *choice* to turn to the dark side. He could have *chosen* otherwise. By turning to crime, he devastated the lives of thousands, including his own family.

Perhaps the only real hope for Cope is to put him away for a very long time. Perhaps his denials would break down, and he'd admit to himself that he's addicted to conning. Maybe he'll turn to the light side again, if he really was ever there.

Then, considering the victims, I realize it's important for Cope to go to prison so that his victims can feel a sense of closure and begin to recover. And there must be restitution. Even if he did return the money, he can never return all he took from us. Going to prison would at least give the victims something, if only the satisfaction that there will be no more psychic vampire attacks or future victims by these psychic vampires for a very long time.

Just as an illustration, I'll walk you through the repercussions of my experience with Cope.

Financial Repercussions

Recovering financially took about eight years. I was lucky; some never recover. I decided to focus on the goals of recovery rather than the pain of the loss, because you get what you focus on.

Our sports car had to go. We replaced it with a little tin can Aerio. It got good gas mileage and it was inexpensive. Luxury spending had to go and I put us on a tight budget. Still it wasn't enough. I refinanced the house, taking out all the equity, but that money wouldn't last forever because it increased our house payment. It was only a temporary fix, so I had to figure out a way to increase income.

By 2002, my husband Bob's dementia became so severe he couldn't be left alone. The stress of the loss rapidly exacerbated his symptoms. I couldn't leave him and go to work because he couldn't care for himself. He had some valuable property in Colorado, which I proceeded to sell. It ended up in another nightmare of greed and lawsuits. That ate up what was intended to be our backup retirement.

Yet by tapping into the 99% world, miracles happened, and I was able to stabilize my situation and recover while making certain Bob was safely cared for in a very good care facility. It looks like I will never retire, but that means I won't be going out in a rocking chair.

Family Repercussions

I lost credibility with my children about my ability to handle finances. One son got upset when I enrolled in a media/publicity summit and said, "Mom, are you sure this isn't another scam? You know you don't know how to handle your money!" While he was the only one who voiced it, I'm sure there were seven other like opinions from my other children. I knew my son spoke out of love and concern, but his remarks were critical and they hurt.

This kind of criticism is one reason why so many victims hide in the woodwork and never tell anyone they've been scammed. I guess criticisms will never cease until everyone gets out of our 1% thinking and its judgmental mindset.

I wish my children had noticed the hard work, ingenuity and good money management skills it took to survive the Cope disaster and eventually come out debt-free, while others committed suicide or filed for bankruptcy. I wish they had noticed how I'd made certain my husband had excellent care while I began a new career. I wished they had noticed that I never asked anyone for a dime; I just began a new career as a writer while others my age were retiring. In their defense, the Ponzi scheme was dramatic and visible while my recovery was quiet and unobtrusive. And they didn't know the reasons behind my self-sabotaging with money. I didn't understand it myself until very recently.

Emotional Repercussions

They could have been much worse if I had allowed it. After a tragedy, people often forget they have a choice: They can either become victims of it, or victorious over it. I chose the latter. However, I had fallen into another thinking error produced by my 1% thinking. In my anger I'd just forged forward and onward to victory and I'd forgotten to allow myself to grieve. Maybe that's because I wasn't very good at it. A virtue can become a vice when overdone. I didn't know it until I watched a You-Tube video I made to tell people how to avoid, or recover, from fraud. The video revealed an angry woman. I had more work to do on myself, so I erased the video and got to work.

Grieving is important, as long as you don't get stuck in it; but blaming only saps your energy and hurts you. It doesn't harm the perpetrator who doesn't know, or care, how you feel. But going after the perpetrators and not giving up until they were in prison, helped me feel less powerless. Writing this book to help others recover from their own adversities helped me recover as well. You always get when you give.

Recalling all the trauma I've been through, I'm amazed I survived intact. I never realized how bad it all was until I wrote everything down for this book—I guess because I never focused on the problems, only the solutions.

I began to wonder: Do con artists ever stop to think about what they might be doing to their victims, or themselves? I think it's unlikely because they have a form of addiction and the thoughts of addicts often don't process through the frontal lobe where the conscience lives. It's a truth I'd learn unexpectedly when reading an Internet newspaper.

Chapter Nine

CON MEN AND MONEY ADDICTION

*Every form of addiction is bad, no matter whether the narcotic be
alcohol or morphine or idealism. [To that list, I'd add money.]*
—**Carl Jung**, founder of analytical psychology

You now know the story of Cope's fraud and the devastation it caused.
The last four chapters are devoted to sharing the valuable insights gained
from the experience.

We'll begin with addictions because con men are addicts. It lends
understanding to how con men can do what they do with no conscience. While
browsing the Web, I came across an Internet article validating my beliefs about
con men being money addicts. Here Dr. Dean Belnap explains just how bad
money addiction really gets. This excited me because I knew Dean well. He and
my first husband, a child psychiatrist, had been partners in a psychiatric practice
years before.

The article contained excellent information about how an otherwise nice
guy or gal could steal the gold out of their own mother's teeth if they needed a
fix. It also validated what my life's experiences had taught me about money as
an addiction.

The article was difficult to understand. Knowing Dean, I took liberties I wouldn't generally take and rewrote the article and simplified the concepts. However, before I used it, I wanted to clear it with him and make certain that, in my effort to simplify, his concepts weren't altered. After a brief conversation on the telephone to make an appointment, I jumped into my gray Aerio and drove east on I-80 then south on I-15 to get to his home in Kaysville, Utah.

After finishing our catching-up conversation on what had happened with our children and our lives in general, it was time to further explain the reason for my visit. Getting right to the point, I said, "I liked your article on money as an addiction so much I took the liberty of rewriting it to make it easier for the layman to understand, Dean. I hope you don't mind. But before I use it, I want to make certain I haven't altered any of your concepts in my translation."

After handing him the article, I watched him carefully. He read it intently, occasionally shifting in his seat, and once or twice I saw his lips turn up in a faint smile. When finished, he leaned over and returned the article with these words: "You've captured the concepts well. You're a good writer."

I heaved a silent sigh of relief and thanked him for taking time to review the article and for not being offended at my boldness in rewriting it.

After shaking my hand, Dean accompanied me to the massive wooden front doors. I stepped over the threshold, very satisfied that I had discovered something valuable that could help explain addiction in a way I'd never heard it explained before.

Now I present my version of Dr. Dean Belnap's scientific explanation about how a money addict's (or any addict's) mind works to allow them to behave in ways they never would behave unless they were after their "fix."

The Anatomy of Money Addiction

Our brain functions in a way that is unique to human beings, processing thoughts in a very sophisticated manner. When a thought goes through the various parts of the nervous systems in the body, it goes last to a sophisticated part of the brain called the *prefrontal cortex,* which has two hemispheres, the left and the right. Both hemispheres process thoughts, each in its own unique way.

The *right side of the prefrontal cortex* evaluates thoughts for their moral value and gets help from what we call the *conscience.*

The *left side of the prefrontal cortex,* after taking advice from the right side, acts as the thought analyzer. In doing so it engages in what psychologists call inner speech or inner dialogue.

The left hemisphere functions like the CEO of our thought life. After analyzing the thought data, the CEO (left prefrontal lobe) sends out orders to the managers (the rest of the nervous system) to perform certain functions the CEO deems necessary.

With both hemispheres working together, decisions are made by considering both the logic and ethics involved, leading to good results. The ability to choose our responses, those that make us free…is a uniquely human gift. To feel the perfection and beauty of this gift, we need to engage another part of our body.

Enter: The Limbic System

This body part is found in the central portion of the brain and it allows us to feel fear and joy. It is our emotional brain. Under optimal conditions, when the prefrontal lobe cortex and the joy emotion of the limbic system are working together, wonderful things can happen. We can feel ecstasy, well being, joy and all the aesthetic feelings at a much higher level than can anything in the animal kingdom.

But…another protagonist can get in the way of this happening—fear.

Under this less-than-optimal condition, when our sensory input is processed through the fear center of the limbic system rather than the joy center, instead of going to the prefrontal cortex for higher processing, it begins to interact with the *basal ganglia.* These are nuclei located at the base of the nervous system. Their purpose is to keep us alive. The basal ganglia preserves and perpetuates life with four basic survival instincts:

- *Self-preservation:* Instinctively we'll fight or flee.
- *Lust:* Instinctive desire for sex is necessary for the perpetuation of life.

- *Bodily appetite:* Instinctively we all have a desire to eat.
- *Fear of death:* Instinctively man will do anything necessary to stay alive.

These instincts are common to both animals and humans.

Danger Ahead!

When the limbic system bypasses the prefrontal lobe and begins interacting with the basal ganglia, it also bypasses reason and ethics; it is now functioning with the basic animal survival instincts.

The basal ganglia is where our 1% thought system, or **ego thought system,** hangs out. Unaltered by higher brain functions, it supports the fear thought system and enables the addict to do whatever it deems necessary to feed his addiction.

Instead of serving the prefrontal lobe cortex to produce feelings of joy, the limbic system serving the basal ganglia begins planting and supporting the seeds for full-blown addiction. Together, they bypass the prefrontal lobe cortex, and all concern about ethics or reason…which, as you know, is exactly how the addict functions, without reason or ethics.

Money, The Often-Overlooked Addiction

Dr. Belnap points out that some addictions are not as obvious as a drug addiction. Much of the human population is addicted to money, which feeds another addiction…the addiction to more. These are people who worship and are ruled by the god "Wantmore."

After having worked in the courts, prisons, halfway houses and with addicted family members, I've observed many addicts and their patterns. Even before Dr. Belnap's validation, I was convinced that con men are addicts, addicted to money and/or more. This is what drives them to behave like sociopaths. A sociopath has no conscience, and neither does an addict in addictive mode.

With the money addict, as well as with other addicts, all bodily functions are changed. The nerve cells in the basal ganglia are affected, creating electrical chaos in the body. An addict, who doesn't die of cirrhosis of the liver, an overdose, or drug-induced accident, will most often die of a stroke, Dr. Belnap's observation and experience revealed.

In the case of Ponzi schemes, I believe many victims are just as money-addicted as the perpetrators. The difference between victim and perpetrator lies in the degree of the addiction and what the person is willing to do, how many people they are willing to hurt to get their "fix." Any money addict loses his freedom to act. They are acted upon by their addiction, becoming victims of it, and thus lose their internal freedom long before they lose their physical freedom to prison.

What master swindler Bernie Madoff said in the courtroom is revealing: "When I began the Ponzi scheme, I believed it would end shortly and I would be able to extricate myself and my clients from the scheme. However, this proved difficult and, indeed, ultimately impossible. And as the years went by, I realized that my arrest and this day would inevitably come."

Chapter Ten

THE LANGUAGE OF THE CON ARTIST: THE LANGUAGE OF SEDUCTION

Handle them carefully, for words have more power than atom bombs.
—British politician, **Pearl Strachan**

Con artists use words to seduce and manipulate for their own gain. In this context, seduction has nothing to do with sex.

The origin of the word seduction stems from the Latin word *sēductiō,* which means to lead astray or apart from. It's really a very simple word, isn't it? However, when spoken with evil intent, a word holds the power to destroy a person, and even the world.

For instance, recall the tragic story of Reverend Jim Jones and his followers. One can only imagine the words he wielded to convince an entire congregation to poison themselves and their children, in Guyana, South America. For this to happen both Reverend Jones and his congregation must have been functioning in their fear-based 1% minds. Jones' scam had been found out and rather than lose his power and control, he was willing to convince his followers to end their lives, and then take his own. Talk about words having the power to destroy!

Words hold power...those we silently utter to ourselves, as well as those we audibly speak to others. Words are powerful because they trigger thoughts, thoughts trigger feelings, and feelings trigger actions. Actions produce the results we experience as our lives. We'll learn more about this when I introduce the *Thought Spiral* and explain how it works.

Understanding Meaning and Value

In simple terms, words are just sounds our mouths produce...until we attach *meaning* to them. For instance, if a Japanese criminal said to you, "If you do not comply with all my wishes, I will kill your family," the words would have no effect, unless you also speak Japanese. However, if the same words were spoken in your language, they'd hold plenty of meaning; you'd be terrified and do anything to avoid having your family harmed.

If I were to offer someone from an indigenous culture a credit card with a $5 million limit and no payments ever due, it would mean nothing to the indigenous person. The concept of a credit card would hold no *value* to an indigenous person, someone who had never seen or heard of a credit card. However, if I were to make the same offer to an American or European, they'd snatch it up in a heartbeat and would trip over themselves running towards the deal, because the concept of credit cards holds both *meaning and value* for them.

When con artists understand the meaning and value society attaches to certain words, they can use them to swindle, manipulate, persuade, control, or harm. Using language in this manner defines the language of *evil*, the language of *seduction*.

Dennis D. Cope used this language of evil to con his fellow church member victims. One example of the way he manipulated language was this: Cope named his investment group the Millennium Group International Inc. To many of Christian faith, the term *millennium* references the time when it is believed Christ will return to earth and usher in a thousand years of peace and prosperity. Cope's use of the word *millennium* kept investors basking in feelings of trust and security, while he deliberately proceeded to financially rape them. While still under indictment for the Millennium Group scheme, Cope became involved in another Ponzi scheme he called Safevest.

Hawthorne's Story "The Birthmark" Reveals the Seductive Power in Words

Throughout literature and history we find con artists using the words of evil and seduction to feed their addictions. American author Nathaniel Hawthorne's short story "The Birthmark" provides a backdrop to illustrate the seductive powers of words, as well as the extent to which addiction can drive human behavior. Hawthorne's main characters, husband and wife Aylmer and Georgiana, find themselves entwined in lives of seduction and addiction, unable to break free.

Aylmer's addiction? Accomplishment. He is a man of science, intellect and perfection. Georgiana's addiction? Her beauty and pleasing others. The combination proves to be lethal.

Georgiana was a beautiful woman with a tiny hand-shaped birthmark on her cheek. Some believed it surely was the mark of an angel's kiss. She has many suitors but a revelation told Aylmer to claim her for his own, and they married. While originally captivated with his wife's unusual beauty, he soon became fixated on the birthmark, and he eventually came to perceive it as a hideous flaw...an intolerable blemish. Being a learned man, a man addicted to accomplishments, Aylmer functioning in his 1% thought system began to obsess about what others might think of him in light of Georgiana's birthmark. Surely a man of his status would find the wherewithal to rectify such an unsightly blight on the face of perfection!

An addictive need for her husband's approval caused Georgiana to be vulnerable to his manipulations. Sensing her vulnerability, he used words of love, mixed with disapproval, to break down her resistance to allowing him to remove the birthmark. He commented on her beauty but shuddered and looked away when his gaze fell upon the tiny red spot.

Aylmer's addiction to his image and to scientific discovery, and the acclaim thereafter, wouldn't allow him to make peace with his perceptions of Georgiana's "flaw," because it gave him an opportunity to feed his addiction to science. He honed in on her *vulnerability*—the need to please him, to be the epitome of perfection for him. Through that need, he could manipulate her into allowing him to experiment on her.

Using Words to Erode Confidence

This unrelenting erosion of a person's self-esteem is exactly what Dan and Cope did when challenged. We've mentioned the incident with Sandra, another victim/member of the group, and what happened when she requested clarification of what they were actually offering in terms of her investment. When Dan replied to her question dismissively, saying, "Well, *everyone else* understands," not only did he strip away her sense of self, but he also put an end to anyone else's questions. When a person goes into self-doubt, they become vulnerable and don't make good decisions. Sandra said no more. She invested.

This is exactly what Georgiana did. As Aylmer, in righteous indignation, grew more distant, she became more pliable. Simultaneously, the erosion of Aylmer's moral compass emerged. Addicted to cutting-edge scientific discoveries and procedures, he gravitated more and more to a willingness to risk Georgiana's life by using untested techniques to rid her of the "deformity." He justified himself as simply working in her best interest.

This is the language of seduction, with the intention to con his wife. His techniques, I suspect, worked much the same on Georgiana as Cope's did on his wife, Dana. Con artists seem to have well-developed skills to hone in on people's vulnerabilities. Georgiana's vulnerability was her intense need to please, which deprived her of the ability to make sound decisions. Dana Cope's vulnerability was also her need to please her beloved husband to the extent that she, also, loses her ability to make sound decisions. Seduced by his illusions, she compromises her ethics and moral standards.

Upping the Ante

Seductive con artists become more and more capable of upping the ante when it comes to satisfying their addictive needs. Aylmer's willingness is reflected in his words to Georgiana when he catches her in his lab. He grabs her arm tightly, and in a rage yells "Go, prying woman, go!"

Cope's desperation is much more evident when someone questioned his practices and integrity. If anyone tried to question Cope, he would silence them by putting them down with words and gestures. Earlier I mentioned one such incident when someone had the courage to ask Cope if he was honest. Rage welled up in his eyes, he paced the floor in quick, angry steps, then spun and faced the group and glared at his questioner as if he were a mere peon having the audacity to question his Godly presence and said in icy measured words, "Would—you—like—your—money—back?" The words pierced our hearts and our confidence like the daggered point of a witch's icicle.

Aylmer knew the risk he took speaking to Georgiana as he did. What if she defied him? Refused to listen to him? But he was willing to take the risk in order to preserve his ability to feed his scientific addiction, hoping that he had broken her spirit enough that she'd have no more resistance, no will to walk away. Ultimately, his *coup de gras* would satiate his addiction—at least temporarily. For addictions are never satisfied; there must always be more, unless and until people seek help and move from their confused 1% thought system to their clear 99% thought system (the real them) and make their decisions from there.

Just as Aylmer took a risk in losing Georgiana's cooperation, Cope took a risk in knowing that his response to refund the man's money might result in his saying, "Yes, I would like my money back." And he also knew that if that happened, other investors would likely say that they, too, wanted their money back. For Cope, though, I think it was just another roll of the dice. He was willing to take the risk. But he pretty much eliminated the possibility that anyone would ask for their money back with his posturing and intimidating verbal and non-verbal language.

Vulnerabilities Prevent 99% Thoughts and Decisions

Sadly, Georgiana recognizes Aylmer's issues and realizes she may not survive the treatment for the removal of her birthmark.

"I might wish to put off this birthmark of mortality by relinquishing mortality itself in preference to any other mode. Life is but a sad possession to those who have attained precisely the degree of moral advancement at which I stand. Were I weaker and blinder, it might be happiness. Were I stronger, I might be endured hopefully. But, being what I find myself, methinks I am of all mortals the most fit to die."

Georgiana's pathetic plight is that she recognizes that she is in a very unhealthy relationship, but living in her fearful 1% world, she lacks the strength, or knowledge, to change the dynamics. Georgiana's fate demonstrates that her life could have been easier had she been less addicted to pleasing and had developed the courage to contact and use her 99% thought system and make her decisions from there. Then she and Aylmer could have led entirely different lives. And surely the lives of Dennis and Dana Cope would have turned out much differently if she had stopped enabling his addiction and taken responsibility for her addictive need to please him.

Both Dana and Georgiana endured to the end, allowing their seducers to ruin their lives. I know this is true, because I once fell victim to the same ploys. Had I heeded the promptings of my inner voice when I got the image of Dennis Cope dressed as a riverboat gambler stuffing aces up his sleeve, how differently this book might have ended! Actually, it would never have been written.

Yet our 99% minds can turn even the worst tragedy into a blessing and, as Isaiah said, "Give to them, beauty for ashes" (Isaiah 61:3). While you're alive, it's never too late to leap out of the hot pot, although it becomes more difficult the longer you wait, for the weaker you become.

Many intelligent people bought into Cope's bizarre promises, such as stating that the money we gave him to invest would never leave the bank. Could you get safer than that? He implied that we were going to reap unbelievable returns on money that was just going to sit there in a vault and, like yeast, keep multiplying. How could that even be possible? It's a question we'd surely have asked ourselves if we hadn't been under his spell, caught in our 1% thinking. Had we just been thinking with our right mind, our 99% mind, Cope couldn't have used his well-developed art of intimidation to keep us under control. He suppressed any doubts or questions aimed at his ethics.

What Is Not Said Can Still Con

Cope's nonverbal language was as effective as if he'd used audible words, for we automatically translate body language into words in our own minds. His golden boy image, his expensive suits, spoke volumes about success. That flamboyant hair, dyed dark and highlighted with a tinge of red, and his ten thousand dollar smile were irresistible. His powerful and commanding ways of speaking wove us right into his spell, his illusion that all was well in Zion with his Millennium Group.

How could you *not* trust a man who had pictures of himself with your church leader, presenting him with $5 million? It just doesn't get any better than this! How could you not trust a man who treats his investors to a Mexican Riviera cruise? All this and more contributed to the illusion that Cope was not only successful in the secular world but also held in great esteem in the religious world.

However, it is important to be aware of this most deadly seductive tactic. We need to understand how this language of evil works to cast a spell on us, separating us from our good sense. *It's not always what is said; sometimes it is what is left unsaid.* Innuendo can pack a wallop.

"The Dead Princess" from Peter Straub's popular horror novel, *Shadowland,* is a beautiful illustration of how the language of evil manipulates by omitting words and concepts. In it, an evil magician used words loaded with meaning to control his apprentice. The magician tells the story of "The Dead Princess" as a warning to his young and compassionate apprentice who seems to be resisting the evil the wizard attempts to teach.

The evil magician needs some way to get the reluctant apprentice under control; he uses language, just as Cope used loaded words to control his victims in a different way—to gain their trust.

In the story, a flock of sparrows come upon a silent palace. Their curiosity piqued, the sparrows determine that "something terrible" must have occurred. They are frightened when they discover that everyone is asleep. "A curse! A curse!"

They discover that the king and queen's daughter has died. Being the empathetic sparrows that they are, they desire to do whatever they can to relieve the couple's great suffering. They seek the aid of the magician to see if he might grant them the favor of restoring Princess Rose's life. And, indeed, he would… with one condition.

"I will do it," said the evil magician. "But you must agree to sacrifice something for it…Will you give up your wings?" Of course no self-respecting sparrow is going to agree to that. The magician then proposes that they relinquish their feathers. "No!" said the sparrows. "Without our feathers we'll freeze in the winter!"

To that, the magician asks for their song. The sparrows agree to sacrifice their song for the life of the princess. Instantly, all is well in the kingdom, all except for the sparrows.

They begin to experience changes: their bodies flatten out, their feathers become skin, and their beaks change into wide mouths. And their voices begin to croak. They've become frogs—croaking, hopping frogs.

What is the message about words in this story? First, as we have stated, it's not just the words that are used that manipulate and control, it's often those that are left out. The magician said he'd trade their song for the favor, but he said nothing about changing them into frogs. But by taking away part of their essence, he transformed them against their will.

Manipulating with Meaning and Value

The second message shows how the wicked magician used this story to assign *meaning* and *value* to words he could later use to control his young, compassionate apprentice. By telling his apprentice the story of the Dead Princess, the magician puts him on notice to beware of compassion, that it comes with a price. Now the magician only needed to say, "Your wings or your song," for he had assigned meaning and value to them. He tacitly controlled his apprentice through fear. The unspoken threat: evil magicians hold and use dark powers for their own purposes.

Do you see any similarities in Aylmer in "The Birthmark" and in Cope's Ponzi scheme approach? Observe how effectively the evil magician uses language to manipulate perceptions and cause the apprentice to see only what he wants him to see.

Cope used language—verbal and non-verbal—to wield power, and he learned to target the *vulnerable*. We've illustrated how he used the intonation of anger in his voice as arrows to deflect questions and to regain control of his audience. In a way, you might say he held his victims under a spell. He had to maintain the upper hand, especially when he was on a slippery slope.

When people questioned Cope, his internal dialogue might well have been, "I will not allow you to stop me from making a killing. I deserve whatever I can get. I will have what I want, and you will believe anything I say! I am in charge here!"

Affinity Fraud Uses Insider Information

Cope had the advantage of being intimately familiar with what held deep *meaning* and *value* to his victims and how they'd react to certain words. He knew how we'd been preprogrammed. As one of us, Cope had access to "insider information." He was well known in the church community. He knew our philosophies of child rearing and our fears that our children might stray as teens. We gave him great trust, because only a man of exceedingly high moral fiber would be granted the position in the church of teaching seminary to our youth! Indeed.

When it comes to the accumulation of wealth and resources, human behavior can become unpredictable, tense, combative, and fearful. The desire for wealth can reduce the most civil of persons to primitive behavior. Many of us made decisions under Cope's beguiling seduction—promises of unbelievable profits. Sadly, they *were* unbelievable. He's the only one who ended up with our money.

Under normal circumstances, none of us would have considered investing in such proposals as Cope made. But there was nothing *normal* about Cope's business ethics. He set his intentions ahead of time, wove his web of deceit, and charmed us with his beguiling spell. He was going to get to the top; in order to do that, he *would* have our money.

Words That "Undo" the Spell

Just as language can be manipulated with the intent to seduce others, language can also create powerful transformations in people's lives. For instance, in the hands of a shaman, priest, or psychologist, language can serve to heal and to empower a person to enter the 99% world.

In Native American custom, the Apache practice ceremonies to heal human suffering. The afflicted are told, "Everything on earth has power to cause its own kind of sickness, make its own trouble. There is a way to cure all these things." Knowing this gives hope and starts the healing process that will relieve the agony of spirit caused by evil. Used properly, the appropriate words bring healing. The ceremony takes place over several days, and includes chanting and singing of words that bring healing. In our modern language we would call it a deprogramming. The ceremony restores the person's ability to see and perceive clearly. It returns harmony, peace and centeredness.

You could say that language can be used as a double-edged sword—for good or evil, to harm or heal. We need to be discerning individuals, to listen to our 99% selves and call a spade a spade when we see it—especially when a riverboat gambler is shoving it up his sleeve!

Because of the power and deep wisdom in "The Birthmark" and "The Dead Princess," I am posting my entire review of "The Birthmark," as well as Patty Karamesines' analysis of "The Dead Princess," from her doctoral dissertation, on my website, RisingFromAshes.net.

Chapter Eleven
LANGUAGE THAT HEALED

*Watch your thoughts, for they become words. Watch your words,
for they become actions. Watch your actions, for they
become habits. Watch your habits, for they become character.
Watch your character, for it becomes your destiny.*
—An anonymous sage

While thoughts become words, words also become thoughts; in this case, thoughts that healed, as you will see in this story. My part in it began with a phone call.

It's the day before Thanksgiving and I'm caught up in holiday preparations. When I hear the phone, I race across the house to catch it before the caller hangs up. I know by the ring it is a long-distance call, probably from a family member. I pick up just in time. The voice on the other end begins to quiver as she speaks my name, then breaks into tears. I feel my muscles in my shoulders tighten, for I recognize the voice. It's the wife of my favorite cousin, Larry. Just about every time I hear from her, it is a crisis involving my cousin. He's an addict.

Her last call, six months before, spun us into a state of shock from which we'd only barely recovered. Larry had taken an intentional overdose of Oxycontin in a suicide attempt. We all rushed to the Utah Valley Hospital in Provo to be with him in intensive care. We were afraid that he only had hours to live and that we would stay to support his wife and children and help make funeral arrangements.

The doctors said he'd swallowed enough Oxycontin to down a horse. Yet he was as strong as a horse and in his better days had the physique of Mr. America. He still had the biggest shoulders I'd ever seen on a man. After several months of dialysis and rehabilitation, he recovered all but his hearing.

Now, hearing his wife's voice on the phone, I know: He'd overdosed again. I felt like someone has jammed a giant syringe into my solar plexus, drained out my life force and replaced it with ice water. I jump in the car and drive to Salt Lake City. All the way down I think about what I might do to help him and finally realize that the only thing I have left is to polish the mirror of his life for him and let him see what I see as his problem, from a non-judgmental position as an observer with a clear mind unaltered by drugs. I stop at my son Byron's house to type Larry a letter.

Letter to Larry

Wednesday, November 25, 2009

Dear Larry,

I was so looking forward to spending Wednesday with you and was saddened to hear that you are in the hospital having made another attempt to take your life. I love you like my own brother and have spent hours pondering what I could best do to help bring you some peace, and I'm about out of ideas.

Nothing any of us have done has worked because ultimately you are the only one who can help you. All I have left is to share what I see as your way out of misery; doing it is up to you.

As bright as you are, just days away from your Ph.D. in psychology, one would think you'd understand what I'm about to say, but you can't see clearly without a clear mind. And it's difficult to see ourselves clearly anyway. When we look in the mirror, we see our left ear on the right side and our right ear on the left side. Life is like that. So it is much easier for me to see clearly because I'm not seeing a reflection of you. I see the real thing and I come from a non-judgmental viewpoint, with a clear mind that has not been damaged with mind-altering substances that only confuse one's thinking.

First I want to reassure you that all your family loves you dearly. But I also know you won't be able to see it until you stop judging yourself and begin to love yourself. Your family is moving away from you because they just don't know what to do for you and can't stand the pain of seeing you suffer without being able to help.

I can tolerate it only because *I don't see you as sick.* I know who you are, Larry. You've simply made some choices that have caused you to lose your connection with the authentic you.

You are a highly evolved spiritual being who came here so in tune with heaven you could see beings from that dimension. But many light beings like yourself with such a refined spirit find it difficult to live in this dense earth energy, and many, like you, turn to substance abuse just to cope. But it is not the answer, for when you take mind-altering substances, you lose your connection to the light world you seek, and dark energies overtake you.

There is an old Native American legend, which says that we all come to earth with a dark wolf on one shoulder and a light wolf on the other, each vying for control over our lives. How can we tell which one will win? *It's the one we feed!*

Here's how you feed the dark wolf.

- Anytime you condemn yourself for your behavior and project those feelings onto us, thinking it is we who condemn and hate you, you are feeding the dark wolf.

- Anytime you get angry with us and make us wrong rather than recognizing your own guilt and forgiving it, you feed the dark wolf.

- Anytime you say or do anything hurtful to yourself or another, you feed the dark wolf.

- Anytime you take drugs or other harmful substances into your body, you feed the dark wolf.

- Anytime you have a negative thought about yourself or anyone else, you feed the dark wolf.

- Anytime you hold grudges, you feed the dark wolf.

- *Anytime you see yourself as the victim,* you feed the dark wolf.

- Anytime you get so self-absorbed that only your needs matter, you feed the dark wolf.

- Any negative, fearful thoughts or actions feed the dark wolf.

When you get angry with other people because of what they do, or don't do, deep inside you know it's you who doesn't like you, and you are projecting those feelings on to all of us who really love you. That's not a judgment, only an observation based on research and experience.

Here's how you feed the light wolf.

- Begin controlling your thoughts. It's the only thing you have control over; its the only thing you need control over, for your thoughts create your feelings, your feelings create your actions, and your actions create the results you're getting in life.

- Guard that mind like you'd guard the gold in Fort Knox. Don't let any dark wolf intruders near it. If you have a negative thought, cancel it and substitute a positive one. For instance, instead of thinking, "I hate that nurse and the shots she gives. They hurt!" call up a thought like this: "I know this nurse is trying to help me and I am grateful for such good care." It's like canceling a word on the computer and replacing it with the one you want. Or, have a nice song ready to sing to distract you from your negative thought.

- Find something to be grateful for in every situation. Behind every seeming tragedy is a gift, if you will look for it. Yes, it's hard but not as hard as what you're enduring now. Your mind is more powerful than an atomic bomb. Use it to heal rather than to destroy.

- Recognize that no one has done anything to you. You created this movie that is your life before you came here to have certain experiences to grow. If you created this life, you can recreate it by making new choices and give it a happy ending. *Again, you can change the movie you call your life to have a happy ending—by the choices only you can make.*

- Recognize that anytime you have a loving thought or do a loving deed, you are feeding the light wolf.

Speaking of choices: Remember, if you keep choosing what you've been choosing, you'll keep getting what you have been getting. Do you like what you've been getting? Are you *willing* to do something different, to stop feeding the dark wolf and begin feeding the light wolf, and allow it to bring you back to sanity and happiness, *the authentic you?* The dark wolf has been in control for a very long time and will fight to keep in control. Call on the light wolf to chase him off the dark wolf; he has the power!

If you are truly *willing* to make the changes, all of heaven will come to your aid.

Here are your choices and the consequences of each choice, as I see them:

- *You can choose to continue doing what you are doing.* Get instant gratification from the drugs when the dark wolf calls. The consequences are you continue to weaken yourself and further lose your own self-respect, create more guilt and lose more and more family support, and finally die an early death. But remember…when you die, you leave your body behind, but your mind goes with you. And it is your mind where the problem lays, not the body. Pain doesn't go away when you die. Pain is in the mind and you take that with you—what do you think evil spirits are; they're spirits with unresolved guilt, fear and pain, who are afraid to move on. Being in misery, they want company.

- *You can choose to commit suicide*—and really do it right and kill your body. Again, let me remind you this doesn't mean your problems are over; your mind goes with you. Suicide is not a solution. It is not only an unwise decision for you, but it would also cause your family inconsolable grief.

- *You can choose to let the dark wolf die from lack of food and begin feeding the light wolf.* Yes, it will be difficult in the beginning, but it will get easier and if you are really ready and willing, as I said, all heaven will come to your aid—as will your family. We've tried giving you everything you think you want to make you happy—money, love, hours of listening to your problems. Has it worked? No! It has never been enough, because you can't fill a dark hole inside with something on the outside, can you? You know that.

You also know the only person who can help you is you. We've all tried. Psychiatrists, psychologists, hospitals, doctors, and nurses—everyone has tried to help you. Has it worked? No. Look at the results. You have to make a new choice to help yourself.

You know if we could do it for you, we would. We have tried!

Anytime you want help feeding your light wolf, feel free to call. But if you want help feeding your dark wolf, don't call, because for me to listen to you to in your negativity is simply enabling you in feeding your dark wolf.

I love you and continually pray that you will choose to let your light wolf help you find the real powerful incredible you and that your dark wolf will meet an early death, death by starvation.

I would suggest one more thing. When you pray, make it this simple prayer and always be in love and gratitude for your blessings when you pray.

God help me to know they will. And give me the courage and strength to do thy will.

Keep this prayer in your heart at all times.

Your loving cousin,

Claudia

After finishing the letter, I got in the car with my son and his family, and we all drove to my daughter Rebecca's house for Thanksgiving dinner. Six of my eight children were there with their families, along with Becky's in-laws, a few college students who were friends of my grandson's, making a grand total of about thirty-six people

After eating and visiting, I gathered several small pieces of the various pies, put them on a large paper plate, covered it with wrap and headed for the hospital, only a few miles away.

As I pull into the parking lot in the hospital complex, I see the psych building is the farthest south in the hospital complex. It's a pleasant-looking new brick building. Entering the building, I wind my way through a maze of hallways and elevators. The closer I get to the psych ward, the colder and more lifeless it feels, especially when I approach a locked door. There is a phone on the wall with a number to dial for an attendant. A few minutes later, an attendant appears and asks me for the code, which I provide. She allows me to enter.

Everything is sterile white yet the energy feels dark and depressing. I see only hallways and locked doors, and I follow the nurse who leads me to one room and unlocks the door. I reluctantly step inside. It's a large room, vacant except for a long table with Formica top and chairs along both sides. Two men are bouncing a ball back and forth to each other. The one dressed in a hospital gown is Larry. My eyes are drawn to his huge shoulders, as always.

I give Larry a hug and sit his pie on the table. He sits down and I sit across from him. As he picks up the fork, his hands are trembling. First I think it might be from withdrawal, but after a few minutes when he realized I wasn't going to scold him or add to his overloaded bucket of guilt, he relaxes and his hands stop shaking.

After he finishes his pie, I hand him the letter, explaining I'd written it because I knew what a difficult time he was having with his hearing. As he finishes the letter, tears well up in his eyes and he says, "I didn't know I was that bad."

I'm a little surprised and more than a little upset by his response.

"Larry, that is not what that letter was about. There is a lot of love in that letter. Look at the paragraph where I tell you I know who you really are! That letter wasn't about judging you; it was about helping you. The judgments are yours about yourself; they are not mine."

He responds, "I guess your family is waiting for you. You'd better get back to them." It's a clever way of telling me he'd had enough of me.

When I return the next day, I'm surprised by his appearance. Dressed and smiling, he tells me he'd thought about that letter all night, and he is going to change, that he and his wife had a good talk and were going to get back together.

After he got out of the hospital, I called him. He said, "The thing that made the biggest difference for me in your letter was when you said you didn't see me as sick. This *made me believe I could change, which made me willing to change, and all heaven has come to my aid.* I can tell you it has been hard, but Jesus Christ has been with me the whole time."

He is now going to the gym regularly, exercising and turning his life around. At Christmas, he called all his sisters and me and wished us a Merry Christmas without one complaint or one victim word and didn't ask for anything from us. It was the first time he'd ever called without complaining or asking for something.

We continue to pray that he will have divine help in maintaining the strength to keep the dark wolf away.

So there you have it. In Chapter 10, we talked about how words can harm, and here you see how they can also heal. Words are powerful because they trigger thoughts and thoughts trigger feelings; feelings elicit action and action produces results, as I will continue to remind you. If you want to change the results you experience as your life, change the thoughts you are thinking.

The words *"I don't see you as sick"* created new thoughts in Larry's mind that opened up the possibility that he didn't have to live his life hooked on drugs. He had always seen himself as ill. He had been an addict for over twenty years.

Now, finally, the conclusion to the Cope story!

Chapter Twelve

ENDINGS AND BEGINNINGS

No river can return to its source, yet all rivers must have a beginning.
—Native American adage

At long last, Dennis Cope's sentencing hearing arrived: April 20, 2009. Once again, I fly to Phoenix and traverse the sidewalks to reach that glass-faced, alert-eyed building.

As I sit on the hard courtroom bench, I think of everything that's led me, and Cope, and everyone involved…to this moment. I think to myself, "Wouldn't it be nice if we lived life on a chalkboard? That way, if we made a mistake, we could easily erase it and start over. But life is more like a felt-tipped marker. You can't erase it. You can cross it out and begin again—but the original mistake never disappears, nor would we want it to or we might lose the lessons it taught. Although, if you are clever, you can turn a minus into a plus with one new stroke of the marker."

Cope can't undo what he has done; he can't go back and be a non-criminal; he can't undo the consequences of his choices. One of those consequences: his life as a free man has ended. In the same way, I can't undo what I'd done; I can't go to my safe deposit box and find my gold, my life savings, still there; it is long gone. Neither Cope nor I can go back and redo the past.

Cope's new beginning is prison. Yet he still has choices. He can choose to make the most of prison, get into a prison program for addicts and transform his life, or he can continue to play the victim, pine away and die.

My new beginning is clear. I've chosen to create a plus from a minus with the stroke of a decision. The remainder of my life will be about writing, speaking and teaching personal empowerment principles that help people avoid becoming victims, or recover if they have been victimized. In hard times, we all need to rethink our lives and face where our old confused 1% thoughts have gotten us. That's the beginning of a beautiful transformation.

My 99% self speaks up: "Every ending is a new beginning, an opportunity to create a better future."

My thoughts ceased as the judge walked into the courtroom; we stood as instructed while the judge entered. This sentencing wouldn't be easy for any of us. Nothing about this experience had been easy.

This April morning of 2009 marked four years since Cope was indicted. Four *long* years. Each time the court set new sentencing dates, I lined up witnesses, as I'd been asked, victims like me, to testify about the harm Cope had done. And each time, the sentencing was postponed.

I was amazed that the key witnesses I kept lining up were so willing to stick with it. They were still experiencing the financial and emotional devastation of being swindled. It took enormous effort to make arrangements to come to court. Some worked three jobs, and getting time off posed a problem. Others had to scramble just to find the money for gas. Still, they were willing to do it —for a year or more. After the fifth or sixth postponement (there were so many, I lost track), I wouldn't even ask anyone to come. Their emotions were too fragile, their situations so tenuous, and I never knew if any court date was real.

Peter Sexton was the U.S. Assistant Attorney in charge of the case. I wanted to shake him and say, "Three months after the plea-bargain I could have had the courtroom full! A year later I could have had it half full, the year after that, a quarter full. Now, four years later, we have only two witnesses, Sandra and me."

I still have difficulty understanding why the U. S. prosecuting attorney would allow all the postponements.

Waiting to be heard

On the flight from Boise to Phoenix, I'd struggled with how to present my court testimony. I'd already testified at the sentencing for Cope's partner. There, I'd told the judge, "To take a man's money, his means of survival on this planet, abuses a man at every level." I'd given examples of how victims had been abused financially, mentally, emotionally and spiritually. I'd presented the research to back it up.

I presented the research that stated, among other things, that the symptoms of being defrauded were the same as being raped. Victims lose both trust in the system that is supposed to protect them and trust in the world around them. They even lose trust in those who are trustworthy. Worst of all, they lose trust in themselves.

I presented evidence to the court that con men are addicts and can't stop conning and need to be kept away from society to prevent future victims. I further informed the courts that, because con men go under-punished, they keep multiplying because for them, crime does pay. I continued to plead for a stiff sentence as an example to would-be criminals that crime no longer pays.

At Bias' sentence, Judge Teilborg pronounced the sentence: seven years in prison. The judge gave the reasons why he'd pronounced that sentence. As he spoke, I knew he had listened carefully to my testimony; two of the four reasons he gave for his decision came from my testimony. He wanted to prevent future victims and he wanted to send a message to would-be criminals that crime doesn't pay.

What more could I now say here at Cope's sentencing without being repetitive? As it turned out, I'd have little time to say anything at all.

Tension in the Courtroom

I rouse myself from my memories. Something is wrong; the energy in the courtroom is tense, even chaotic. The judge and attorneys are scurrying around as if a crisis were imminent. Then they all disappear into the judge's chambers. The rest of us wait, trying to determine what's going on.

Someone whispers, "I think Cope's mother is having a seizure!"

I don't want to do it, but I can't help thinking, "Is this another con job?"

Finally, the judge and attorneys reappear without any explanation for their absence. U. S. Attorney Sexton walks over to Sandra and me and says, "You'll have to cut your testimonies short." No apology, no explanation.

I bristle inside. Again the needs of the criminal had taken precedence. We'd waited for eight years and put thousands of hours of work into reaching this day. Now we're being denied the chance to tell our full stories, to be heard at last. And there is nothing we could do about it.

The sentencing begins. Cope's attorney pleads with the judge to spare his client from prison, arguing that incarceration would serve no purpose. It's a flimsy argument, easy to rebut, but Cope had no real defense. The argument stands.

Next Up...

An anorexic-looking man who has been wedged between his two hefty lawyers. This man is only half the size of the formerly robust Cope. He looks even smaller and shabbier than he did at his indictment, with gray-blond hair brushing his shoulders and deep vertical crevasses in his saggy face. His down-turned lips bear no resemblance to the confident, even smug grin he once wore. His appearance reveals a man who had become a victim of his own addictions.

In his orange jail pants and green top, arms and legs shackled, Cope shuffles to the microphone. Using his right hand to hold up his sagging jail pants, he addresses the court with his sacred underwear drooping below his right sleeve.

I see nothing that that even faintly represents the Cope I once trusted...until he speaks in his own defense. I expect to hear a weak voice commensurate with his feeble body and so I'm shocked to hear the old Cope voice coming from this new person.

While listening to his smooth, flawless speech, still manipulative and powerful, I'm stunned to find myself struggling to maintain my objectivity. He still has that same seductive, hypnotic ability. Then the words of the *Forbes* writer Dirk Smillie pop into my head to save me. I had asked him how he would profile a con man, and he said, "Con men live in an alternate state of reality which is more fiction than fact, and they come to believe their own lies."

It's their belief in their own lies that makes them convincing, I remind myself. Because they believe their own lies, their lies seem believable. They are addicts and can't be trusted. My objectivity returns. I remain steadfast and resolute in my purpose.

As Cope continues, he makes reference to friends whom he believes have betrayed him—a classic example of denial and projection. I know he's trying to manipulate me into softening my testimony. I am again reminded of what a convincing and seductive con artist he is, and even more convinced of how badly the unsuspecting public needs to be protected from him.

Supporting the Con Man

Whether to manipulate the courts or because of genuine physical limitations, Cope's stepfather—stooped, walking slowly—makes his way to the witness stand. He belabors the fact that he's been laid up with poor health, and says he desperately needs his stepson's help.

"It's all a con," I think. I hate being so suspicious!

Cope's mother is up next and it's more of the same. She looks like a homeless waif and, whether it's real or feigned, she speaks with a pathetic voice, telling the court how much she needs her Denny because she is ill and having seizures. She pleads in her child-like voice, "Denny is such a good son and I really need him."

I can't help myself; I roll my eyes.

Finally, Dana takes the stand.

I can best describe her as another walking contradiction. Her dull blonde hair falls straight to her shoulders, but the strands don't fit together smoothly. Her attire is a cross between modern granola and Vegas showgirl—an earth tone crocheted skirt and dark glittering high heels. She speaks in a whimper, her words broken by sobs and tears as she dabs her eyes with a tissue. She begs the judge not to put her wonderful and beloved husband in prison, because he is such a *good* man.

Generally I'm compassionate, but her words have no impact. I see her as the classic enabler/addict, responsible for enabling her husband to maintain his addiction. She is manipulating; manipulation and addiction go together like bread and butter.

As much as I'm offended by this display of emotion and irrational thought, I'm equally distressed with myself. I've lost my ability to see the best in people. I miss my innocence. I miss being able to trust people. Cope stole more than my money.

Our Turn

Sandra was a seventy-year-old woman now stooped with age, who should have been retired, but once she'd lost her money to Cope, had to keep working on the hard cement floors of her cookie company. On the stand, she spoke of the trials she'd been through with her husband's health as a result of losing their money.

She tried to cut her testimony short, as requested, but it still wasn't short enough for the prosecuting attorney. He rises and walks up to the witness podium, interrupting Sandra's testimony, to tell her to...cut it shorter. She finishes with, "Cope is a wolf in sheep's clothing!"

Then it was my turn.

I was glad my testimony followed the Copes. I had been able to maintain my objectivity, enabling me to logically overcome some effects of the drama, and paint a more accurate picture of this conman supreme, who lived off the blood and sweat of other people's labor, who still lives off our labor, using our money for his high-priced attorneys, and our tax money to pay his board and room—in prison.

I told the judge, "I have bird-dogged this case for eight years, for one reason only—not out of revenge or hatred for Cope, but to protect future victims, which there will surely be if this man is not put away for a very long time. Yet he says he's learned his lesson. Has he? We know he became involved in another Ponzi scheme while still under indictment for this one. Cope can't stop conning. He's an addict."

I'd covered the physical and mental trauma the fraud had created at Bias' sentencing, so I reminded the judge of the emotional abuse victims suffered. I talked about things that traumatized us, the "friends in high places" threat, the mysterious death of our original attorney and the mysterious disappearance of others working the case…I felt tension grip the room as if I had uttered forbidden words.

Then I too got the "shorten it further" request right in the middle of my testimony. I left the stand with so much more to say.

Sentencing at Last

This is what I recall: Before pronouncing the sentence, Judge Teilborg deferred to Sexton for his recommendation for a sentence: Sexton hesitated for some time, then asked the judge to determine the sentence. *Why all the hesitation about imposing a sentence?* I wondered. Had all the drama reached its target?

The judge read excerpts from the victim letters and again emphasized the importance of keeping Cope from harming others with his habitual need to con. He stressed the need to send a message to would-be criminals that crime doesn't pay. Then the judge pronounced Cope's sentence.

Seven years.

This is a very heavy sentence for a white-collar crime, which generally goes under-punished.

Cope's mother gave an encore performance and had another seizure. (Sorry to be cynical. I *really* don't like being like that way—oscillating between compassion and anger—it's the anger I detest the most. Yes, Cope did steal more than our money!)

Court dismissed. The prosecuting attorney, Peter Sexton, rushes out of court. Weeks ago, he'd promised to meet with me after the sentencing and answer all my questions. But he brushes me aside, explaining that he has another case to attend. He points to his assistant, saying, "You can talk to him."

I'm speechless; I can't even respond. I felt like I had been dismissed right along with the case, swept away like dirt in a dustpan. I had so looked forward to the meeting with Sexton! Could he ever understand what this case meant to us? I had put so much into it, yet I wasn't offered the courtesy of even one answer out of the many that had been promised.

Conning the Courts

Cope and his family had wrapped themselves in the mantle of victim, another clever way of manipulating the court's perception. Con men just never stop conning. It seems the court bought the manipulation and forgot who the real victims were. I so wanted to be grateful for all the work they had done in bringing this case to a close but gratitude wasn't easy to come by when I was feeling re-victimized. I couldn't change the outcome of this case. Later I'd work to make changes in the system. Now there was nothing left to do but go home.

Leaving the courtroom, I enter the elevator with several others. Its doors close with finality as it swallows us up and deposits us on the first floor. Walking past security to the huge glass doors that empty the contents of the building onto the street, I feel the energy of something vicious and angry behind me.

Dana's Last Words

"Some people are liars, vicious liars." I hear the angry, yet weak, voice behind me; I turn to see…Dana Cope. Knowing the words are targeted at me, I'm surprised by my calm response and the desire to leave her with something to help her.

"That's classic denial and projection," I answer calmly.

Although I doubt any of it sunk in, I hope the words will come back to her later and mean something.

"I'm not talking to you," she snaps.

Knowing her words are spoken from a place of denial, I again respond calmly, "Well, I am talking to you."

The conversation ends there.

Stepping out of the massive glass doors onto the paved courthouse entry, I pull out my cell phone to call a cab to the airport. All the while, I'm thinking back to my strange exchange with Dana.

My ego again steps in, as I say to myself, "Why didn't you just call her a pathetic deluded woman and tell her that, as an accomplice to her husband, instead of standing there blubbering, she should be thanking her lucky stars she's not in prison too?"

It's a good thing I didn't. I might have ended up in a fistfight. My 99% mind reminded me that I didn't really want to hurt her; she was already hurting enough.

Thinking about how much she'd lost when she bound herself to Cope and all his schemes, I remembered an earlier encounter—on a cruise.

Torn Inside

When we were not getting the return on our money as promised and promised and promised, enough people started muttering that Cope's credibility began to suffer, so he booked his victims on a three-day cruise. It was a clever ploy to regain our "*con*fidence." On that cruise, Dana and I struck up a conversation that—of course—came around to her husband. Her expensively highlighted hair gleamed and her pampered skin glowed. "I love him sooo much," she confided as the ship gently rocked beneath us. And she did. She loved him sooo much, she apparently couldn't see that he had done anything wrong.

In truth, she was his accomplice. In implicating him, she would have to implicate herself. Maybe that's why she couldn't see the truth. She couldn't face it and began to live in a make-believe world instead. I pondered the ways addictions rob one of free choice and how con men become victims of their own addictions as do their families and of course, all of the other victims.

On the plane home, I could hardly speak a word. My mind was occupied. I was hurting and humbled by the events of the day. I thought the day would be a triumphant conclusion to the eight-year saga, yet I felt no satisfaction. I sensed that I couldn't…until I learned the lessons I knew were hidden behind this tragic situation…and all tragic situations.

In the end, we were considered amazingly successful by the standards of our 1% ego thinking, which screamed, "Yes...we won! We put them in prison!"

But my 99% self didn't rejoice. It knew the damage everyone had sustained. Some were still recovering. Some never would recover; they were dead. Yet my deeper motives had been satisfied. I take comfort in knowing Cope and Bias can victimize no more for at least fifteen years or so (after they are sentenced for other pending Ponzi schemes). But the comfort is dulled by pain as I realized I'd solved the problem, to some degree, with the same level of thinking I was at when I created it. Still I could turn that minus into a plus with another stroke of my pen, and I would.

All I could focus on at the moment was the nauseating recognition that Cope's addictive desire for more had not only physically killed and psychologically maimed hundreds, even thousands of people, but he had also brutally victimized himself and his own family.

Still I remember his pathetic words spoken in court, the only ones that ever rang true: "I never meant for anybody to get hurt." I believe he never really meant to hurt anyone. His addictive desires marched right past his frontal lobe, where the conscience lies, grabbed the hand of the limbic system and together they marched straight for the basal cell ganglia that housed his animal survival instincts.

For days after I returned home, I felt lethargic and I developed a bad case of laryngitis. I'd awake in the middle of the night with my whole gut feeling like it was being churned with an eggbeater. Although I desperately wanted the case to be over, something about it wasn't finished. My soul cried out to understand why. I hungered for a peaceful conclusion, for some closure to the eight-year drama. It sickened me to think about how this thing we call money—this thing humans invented simply as a convenient means of exchanging goods and services—could create so much pain for so many people.

This is the world we've created with our confused 1% thoughts!

How did our 1% world become so powerful? How did our 1% thinking about money become so distorted that it creates such horrendous social problems? What can we do about it?

The answers came slowly. Eventually, I found life-changing truths about money and life to help victims heal and prevent others from becoming victims. But I would soon learn that my most important work lay ahead. My new task: transforming all those frustrations, feelings and emotions into something positive. I was certain I'd find a way to create beauty from ashes. My work in Phoenix was complete.

New Resolutions

The hardest work was yet to come. While the wounds have healed, it will require surgery to remove the ugly scars that separate me from my soul. I know, once they are removed, I'll be able to step out of my victim shoes and, like the mythical Phoenix, rise from the ashes.

I've spent too much time in the 1% world. I've resolved to spend more time in Einstein's world, the place where we solve all our problems. I've lived far too long at the level where we create them.

Resolved: This is my new beginning. My new river of life will flow in a different direction.

I've opened my soul and shared my story for only one purpose, to vividly *illustrate* the pain, suffering, anger, and chaos created by living an ego-based life.

I've opened my soul and shared my story to show you the kinds of thoughts, the mental mindset that I, and others, were entertaining throughout this traumatic ego experience and what it created.

I shared it because it's only when you begin to see the damage we do to ourselves with this 1% thinking that we have a desire to find something better. And when you find it, you'll recognize it, because you have something to compare it to.

In Sections Two and Three, you'll find something to compare it to, outcomes, even miracles, created by our 99% thinking. Notice the difference in the mindset, the thinking patterns of those in the stories in Section Two compared to the mindset of those in Section One.

What have we learned about the 1% mindset? I'll summarize:

- *Money is more important than life itself:* the message of the suicides
- *Enough is never enough:* the message left by those who already had enough to live a comfortable lifestyle but wanted more.
- *Life is a battlefield:* it's me against you; for me to win, you have to lose; our lawyers against theirs—the message of the court battle
- *Solving problems with 1% thinking provides lose-lose solutions:* Victims lost their money, their health and their lives. Cope and Bias lost their freedom; others lost their sanity.

Why do we tolerate it? Maybe it's because we are like the frog in the pan of warm water in which the heat gets turned up a degree a day. The frog adjusts and hardly notices until one day—it is dead, floating in the pan of boiling water. Maybe that is what is happening to so many who die too young with cancer and other diseases. Maybe the internal heat from all of the above pressures and ugly ego interactions cause our body to take us out a few cells at a time until one day, there aren't enough healthy cells left and our body stops—dead.

Maybe it is because we've gotten soft. Life has been too easy. We've gotten accustomed to having the luxury of sitting around reading the slicks and popping grapes, or escaping from life in the boob tube.

Maybe we're too busy working frantically to keep up with the Joneses to notice.

Maybe we close our eyes and tolerate the pain because we see no way out. If that is the case for you, here's the good news. There *is* a way out!

The "way out" of what we call the "Real World" is revealed in the following two sections. You've already discovered some clues in this section such as:

Clues to Recovery

- Use a "holographic" approach—looking at a problem from many different angles—to discover and overcome vulnerabilities.

- Recognize that a 1% solution (court battle) to a 1% problem (Ponzi scheme) is ultimately a lose-lose for everyone.

Here are more clues:

- Grieve, don't blame. Blaming only saps your energy.
- Make a choice. Will you remain a victim or become a victor?
- Focus on the solution, not the problem.
- Work your solution until it manifests.

We are now leaving this "real world"—our confused, ego-thinking 1% world, the world of heart attacks, ozone cracks and psychic vampires. Next, we'll transcend this dark ego world through fascinating stories that unravel deeper mysteries and deeper truths about wealth, abundance and genuine peace and happiness. This is the world of 99% living.

Update on Cope as of 2-4-11
Inmate Locator - Locate Federal inmates from 1982 to present

Name	Register #	Age-Race-Sex	Release Date	Location
DENNIS D COPE	09527-073	58 White-M	12-08-2014	NOT IN BOP CUSTODY (Bureau of Prison)

I called the attorney in California who is prosecuting Cope in the second Ponzi case he got involved in while under indictment for ours. She offered little information. Although he did plead guilty in this case, he will not be sentenced for another year (Provided he is in a local jail or prison in California waiting for sentencing in his second offense.)

I called the FBI in Arizona to inquire about his location. I have gotten no response. I emailed him at the same address I used previously. His email came back, undeliverable

I called and emailed the prosecuting attorney in Arizona and asked him the same question. I've gotten no response.

Then I finally heard from the FBI. FBI Harold explained that Cope was in a California facility.

Then we checked again to see what the register showed. Here's what we got the second time.

Here's a March 6, 2011 report from the inmate locator:

Inmate Locator - Locate Federal inmates from 1982 to present

Name	Register #	Age-Race-Sex	Release Date	Location

Inmate Not Found. (Printed in bold Red)

Name: COPE DENNIS **Race**: White **Sex**: Male

Again I contacted the FBI to see what had happened. I needed an explanation to why there is no registration #, no release date, and no location listed for Cope now. I also needed an explanation for the words Inmate Not Found posted in big bold red letters. They simply report he is a white male and appear to have no idea where he is.

To date, two months after my inquiry, I have received no response. I'll give the FBI the benefit of the doubt. I'm sure they are busy with all the increased crime. And maybe the BOP is not efficiently or regularly posting to the Inmate Locator.

Yet again I ask the same question that has plagued me for now nearly ten years, *"Does Cope have friends in high places?"* If so, who? If so, why would they protect him? What do you think?

Section Two

EXPERIENCING A
BETTER WORLD

God turns you from one feeling to another and teaches by means of opposites so that you will have two wings to fly, not one.
— **Mevlana Rumi**, 13th century Sufi poet and mystic

After experiencing the 1% world of the Ponzi scheme, it becomes clear that it is a world we don't want. Next, we will experience its opposite, the 99% world, the world we all deeply desire. By discovering this world through stories, we find the second wing we need to fly.

Through stories everything is made possible.
— **Yellowman**, a Native American sage

Introduction

BEYOND THE FIVE SENSES

The extent (proportion) of the known world as compared to the subtle world or subtle dimension is 1 to Infinity. Absolute knowledge, also known as divine knowledge, is that which is complete, totally authentic and does not change, or is ultimate...[it comes from the subtle world].
—**Spiritual Science Research Foundation**

The information in this section will help you tune yourself to your subtle 99% world. When reading the stories, consider what the individual or individuals who received 99% information were trying to accomplish. What were their motivations? Were they seeking to aggrandize or glorify themselves, or were they acting for a higher purpose?

Likewise, consider your own motivations. When trying to tap into this world, what you are trying to accomplish? Are your desires and motivations similar to those who actually have connected to that world?

There are many frequencies out there from which we can pick up information external to our five senses. They are not all frequencies we want to tune into. So how can we tell if we are tuned into the frequency where all Truth is found?

To connect to the 99% world, you must be on the right wavelength. You can't tune into the FM LOVE channel and find Truth if your fearful negative thoughts have you tuned into the AM FEAR channel. Therefore, we have donated an entire section of this book to share the metaphysical and scientific principles by which you can tune out of the AM FEAR station, which broadcasts only confusion, and tune into the FM LOVE station.

In addition to what you'll learn in Section Three, it is also very useful to relax your body and quiet your mind through meditation as you attempt to tune into the FM LOVE station.

To fully connect to this world, you need to be thinking loving thoughts, feeling loving energy and acting in loving ways. This is vital.

Chapter Thirteen

MONEY IS LIKE WATER

The love of money may be the root of all evil. What I know
for certain is this: Love of money is the root that feeds ego.
— **The author**

Our ego is simply our fear-based thought system, our confused 1% minds at work. If you think about it long enough, you'll find that nearly all of our thoughts around money are fear-based: fear about not having enough, fear of losing what we have, fear of having less than the Joneses. Fear-based thinking about money enables fraud and creates victims. This fear of "not enough" nourishes the roots of ego and keeps it alive and well. If we're going to transform our ego-based, fear-based thought system, we must address our issues about money.

One breakthrough about money came to me at the famous Sun Valley, Idaho, resort—home of movie stars, excellent skiing, and a strong spiritual movement. I was there to attend the yearly Wellness Seminar.

There I was introduced to the story of Gertrude, a story that taught me the deepest and most significant lessons on money I've learned thus far in my journey. Gertrude was poor in money but rich in spirit. She was neither addicted to money nor run by ego. Who better to teach this lesson?

I almost missed it. My friends wanted me to have breakfast with them at 9 a.m. at the lodge. But I'd noticed earlier that a woman named Lynne Twist, with an organization called the Hunger Project, would be giving a speech about fundraising at the same time. I knew nothing about her or her organization and had little to no interest in fundraising. My 1% brain urged me to go to breakfast instead. Yet something deep inside whispered, "Go to the lecture."

By then, experience had taught me when my inner voice speaks in pictures or words, I pay a high price when I don't listen. The best example: when I ignored the image of the riverboat gambler as I first heard Cope speak.

At the lecture, I settled into my seat just as Lynn took the stage: an attractive woman, with dark neck-length hair and a slim build. Mostly I noticed her lovely, sincere smile and felt her positive energy. Her words truly came from the heart and my heart was touched. As she shared the experiences that influenced her life, I realized that she had the healthiest perspective on money I've heard. I could see why she was in demand in over forty countries to teach people how to raise funds for their organizations. I'm very surprised that a person who did fundraising would have this effect on me. I'd always seen them as overly aggressive, a sort of nuisance that needed to be avoided.

But the stories she told about her experiences with the poorest and the richest on the planet and what she had learned from each of them opened a space for me to look at my own skewed relationship with money and how it influenced me to become involved in the Ponzi scheme.

Lynne described seeing people both destroyed and healed by money and shared how those experiences shaped her own perspective on money. I became aware of my own flaws, and those of our entire society, in thinking about money; I became aware of the illusions and attachments created by these thinking flaws as well as the disastrous consequences that have resulted. Lynne looked at money from an entirely different perspective than anyone I'd ever met. It was those we would call the poor, including the indigenous people she worked with, who gave her the higher insights into money. She passed on to us some lessons she'd learned, which I now pass on to you.

One story in particular struck my heart. It involved two very different people: a financially struggling maid and a wealthy CEO.

Lynne had a minister friend who asked her to come to his church in Harlem and speak to his congregation about her newly started Hunger Project. She agreed and flew to New York immediately after another fundraising meeting in Chicago. Her plane was delayed due to weather and when she finally arrived in Harlem, over an hour late, she found everyone still waiting patiently for her arrival.

The church was in the basement of an old building. Water was leaking through the roof and walls of the room; the most prominent sound in the room was the plink, plink, plink of the water dropping into the buckets. She realized this tiny congregation would have little to give to her fundraising effort.

She walked to the pulpit to speak about the Hunger Project. She was the only white face in the room and she felt, in her words, "officious and silly" in the silk dress she'd worn to impress the CEO she'd met with earlier that day. She described the Hunger Project's work and goals and then came the moment to ask for donations. She looked at the audience; the CEO she'd met earlier probably spent more on his suit than any one of them made in a month. She looked at the many buckets strategically placed to catch the dripping water. She hesitated, hands sweating, wondering if asking for money was the right thing to do. She went ahead and made the request, which was met with absolute silence.

Finally, a woman sitting towards the back stood up. She looked to be in her late sixties or early seventies, her gray hair parted down the middle and swept up neatly into a French twist.

"Girl," she said to Lynne, "my name is Gertrude and I like what you've said and I like you. I ain't got no checkbooks and I ain't got no credit cards. To me, money is a lot like water. For some folks, it rushes through their life like a raging river. Money comes through my life like a little trickle. But I want to pass it on in a way that does the most good for the most folks.

Gertrude's Gift

Gertrude continued, *"I see that as my right and my responsibility and my joy. I have $50 in my purse that I got from doing a white woman's wash, and I want to give it to you."*

Gertrude walked down the aisle and handed Lynne her $50 in crumpled bills, then gave her a big hug. As Gertrude headed back to her seat, other people came forth to make their contributions in five-, ten- and one-dollar bills. Lynne opened her brief case to act as a sort of basket to collect the money.

As each person arrived at the briefcase and deposited their money, Lynne recognized the true spirit of giving, and tears pooled in her eyes. It seemed as if they all were participating in a sacred ceremony, acting with a deep integrity of the heart. Lynne watched as the hard-earned bills slowly covered the $50,000 check she had obtained from her previous meeting, hiding it from sight.

Gertrude's money was infused with the spirit in which Gertrude had given it, the commitment to make a difference. She felt it was "blessed money," and so it was.

This is how Lynne described Gertrude's gift: "The precise amount of the money and how much it would buy was secondary to the power of the money as it moved with purpose, intention and soulful energy in the act of contribution. Gertrude taught me that the power of money is really derived from the intention we give it and the integrity with which we direct it into the world. Gertrude's gift was great and her clarity helped me regain my own."

Gertrude's story should help any open mind gain clarity about money. She and her fellow congregants lived in humble circumstances, but their relationship with money had not become fear-based; it remained love-based, something we rarely find in more affluent areas of society. What a powerful demonstration that poverty is not a condition but a state of mind!

This is not the end of Gertrude's story.

After she left the congregation, Lynne's mind again turned to the $50,000 check that lay buried beneath all the precious bills in her briefcase. She couldn't help but contrast the feelings she had in this church with those she'd felt, only hours ago, when she'd obtained the check.

She had met with the CEO of a successful company based in Chicago. His office had the trappings of a powerful executive: a massive desk, a huge window with a skyline view. The CEO sat behind the desk.

Lynne sat down opposite him, trying and failing to see his face through the glare flooding through the window behind him. She gave her presentation, finishing with a request for funds to support the Hunger Project.

The man didn't say a word. Without any comment about her presentation or her project, he opened his desk drawer, pulled out a check for $50,000—already written and signed—and offered it to her. She accepted it, put it in her briefcase, and left for New York.

Throughout her flight, she was troubled by the man's response. His absence of emotion left Lynne feeling hollow, empty. She was sure he hadn't heard much of what she said and didn't care at all about the Hunger Project. Yet he'd already decided to donate. Why? She was so upset, she began to cry. She couldn't understand why the whole experience had made her feel so badly.

After Lynne met Gertrude, she got it.

His company had recently made some unethical business decisions and gotten a lot of bad press. This donation was intended to buy some good press. This money was infused with guilt. She'd felt it but didn't know how to define it until Gertrude taught her that money, like water, is a carrier. Lynne said, "It can carry blessed energy, possibility and intention, or it can carry control, domination and guilt. It can be a current or currency of love—a conduit for commitment—or a carrier of hurt or harm."

Of course, Lynne cried after she took the check. Her 99% mind knew what it carried, even before Gertrude brought forth that truth. We are all such a gift to each other if we would be non-judgmental and recognize the gift. Now, after listening to Gertrude and experiencing the outpouring of love from this little congregation, she knew the CEO's money, in contrast to theirs, was "dirty money," a bribe. She could feel it and began feeling even worse about taking it.

Lynne knew she had to return the guilt money.

A Right Decision and Its Reward

She sent the check back with a carefully worded letter, explaining that she could tell the CEO didn't have his heart in the project and suggesting that he consider giving the money to a project for which he had some feeling.

In the next few years, the Hunger Project grew and became very successful and garnered much positive press. Unknown to Lynne, the CEO followed her organization's work. After he retired, he contacted Lynne and told her he was very impressed with what she had accomplished. Now he was ready to make a donation from his heart. He handed her a check for $200,000.

He told her that he hadn't even remembered giving her the check, but he never forgot the letter that accompanied it when she sent it back. He began to re-evaluate his perspective on money, to think about life differently and use his money to bless rather than manipulate.

Perhaps he considered the words of Mohandas K. Gandhi who said, "Capital as such is not evil; it is its wrong use that is evil. Capital in some form or other will always be needed."

Maybe he considered the words of Thornton Wilder, who said in *The Matchmaker,* "Money is like manure; it's not worth a thing unless it's spread around encouraging young things to grow."

Lynne's conviction, courage, and example caused this man to look deeply into himself and to begin thinking with his wise 99% mind. Is it not a wonderful thing that man is endowed with the magnificent capacity to change his life by changing his thinking?

And it was all prompted by Gertrude's example.

> *"The direction of the mind cannot help but be determined*
> *by the thought system to which it adheres. The thought system*
> *of the Holy Spirit is guided by love, the thought system of the*
> *ego is guided by fear, [guilt] and hatred, and will*
> *always eventually result in some kind of destruction."*
> — From A Course in Miracles

Without conscious thought and effort, the mind will take the path of least resistance, the default path...downward. Our focus on the need for more, our fear of loss and deprivation, leads to that downward path. It is the root cause of dishonesty, murder, and lies—the root of all evil.

Money itself has the meaning we give it. So many of us have allowed it to become an all-consuming monster. It becomes "good or evil," depending on whether our ego 1% thinking or our higher 99% thinking takes over. The choice is ours.

Chapter Fourteen

MIRACLE IN THE DESERT

I learned early on that if change is to occur,
one must be willing to think and do the unthinkable.
— **Toni Morrison**, first African-American author
to win the Nobel Prize for literature

In a forgotten sandy desert at the western tip of the African continent live a people who are so remote and so disconnected from society that their own government doesn't even recognize them. Yet from this indigenous tribe of Senegalese Muslims, we learn what it takes to create miracles—for they were willing to do what for them, for centuries, had been unthinkable.

The following story is powerful. It is true. And it shows what can be accomplished by those who appear to be desperate and powerless, once they move to a different level of thinking. The story revolves around a small group of quiet women in this resourceless community who tap into their hidden inner powers and save the lives of men, women and children in seventeen desert communities.

The Story...

In the remote village of Senegal, far away from the bombardment of the many chaotic voices of our modern society that shout so loudly in our ears, is a remarkable village of people who live protected from these disturbing voices, which, in our culture, drown out the helpful ones.

Yet these people also have their problems. They are still stuck in old traditions that, had they remained unchallenged, could have kept them from tapping those inner resources so readily available to them and could have cost them their lives.

We have this story because Lynne Twist and her group of Hunger Project workers went to this remote village, where they would learn that in order to help the people there, they'd have to encourage them to do the unthinkable— challenge their sacred traditions. And in doing so, they would create a miracle for their village and sixteen other villages in this remote desert.

The wisdom of this delegation lay in recognizing that the best form of help is to help the villagers help themselves and not simply give them a handout. On another mission, the Hunger Project workers had seen the damage done by well-meaning but unwise givers in a section of Bangladesh, where because of the overabundance of charitable handouts, they have lost their ability to provide for themselves and are totally dependent on outside resources for their sustenance. They have gained a global reputation for being needy and helpless. Once these people began to identify themselves as helpless, losing touch with any sense of their own competence, they saw themselves and their country as incapable of success.

Not only did the delegation feel it unwise to give the Senegalese a handout— these people didn't want a handout. They didn't see themselves as victims. By helping these people help themselves, this delegation did them a beautiful favor, never knowing their gift in return would be to witness the Senegalese create a miracle, one the Hunger Project delegation would never forget.

Senegal is a small coastal country on the Horn of Africa. Historically it was a French slave-trading colony. Castles of the slave owners with their prison-like dungeons still dot the land today, now tourist attractions and sad reminders of the inhumanities of man to his fellow man.

Much of Senegal consists of the massive Sahel desert. As its fine orange sand crawls ever closer to the sea, it deposits itself over everything in its path: plants, roads, houses, and even villages. Desert living is harsh, an environment in which water is scarce and precious. And for the past few years, water had been harder and harder to find. Their water was running out, and if they didn't discover a new supply soon, their people would perish.

The Hunger Project heard about the plight of these forgotten desert dwellers and faced this awesome desert to see what they could do to help. At first the trip seemed like a grand adventure, yet as they drove deeper and deeper into the desert itself, the delegates too became covered with the fine sand, feeling it burrow deep into their lungs with every breath. The adventure began to feel more like an exercise in endurance. Going on, they found fewer and fewer people, fewer plants and fewer signs of animal life.

After driving into the orange wind for some time on a rough, unpaved road, the road disappeared into the sand. The driver pulled out his compass and continued the journey, driving now by compass only. The Senegalese drivers knew the desert and knew when it was time to stop, turn off their engines and wait for the faint sound of drums. First came a faint, almost imperceptible, noise that grew louder, revealing the direction from which it originated. The drivers again turned on their engines and proceeded towards the sound of the drums, which grew louder and louder. They passed two huge trees, and the drivers explained these are Baobab trees, precious desert trees that require very little water and provide copious amounts of shade and also act as a windbreak from the high desert winds.

Finally, on the horizon, they see tiny specks moving towards them. Soon the specks transform into dozens of children running toward the vehicles, bubbling with excitement. The group reaches the vehicles and some children jump into the cars for a ride, others run alongside the cars, still others, including the men and women, stand on the sidelines, cheering, clapping, dancing, shouting and drumming, acting as the greeting committee to welcome their delegation of eighteen.

The cars stop. Climbing out of their automobiles, moving closer to the people, they notice dozens of women wearing beautiful colorful *boubous*: long, loose, colorful Senegalese dresses with headdresses to match. The atmosphere is festive; drums are beating, children are shouting, women are squealing with delight, men are singing. It's a welcome you'd be hard-pressed to find anywhere in America. As the celebration continues, the villagers draw the delegation closer. Time seems to stand still as they dance and sway as one.

Suddenly, the drums and festivities stop; it's time for business. Using a translator, the chief explains that their village is several kilometers away, further explaining that they have come to welcome the delegation and are grateful for the *partnership*.

These proud people aren't looking for a handout, expecting to stand back and let this little delegation care for them; they want a partnership. They see themselves as a strong and able people and were willing to work to help themselves, but realize they are limited. They are proud of their spiritual home, the desert, yet they realize they need help to find water, or life for them and sixteen other villages cannot continue. And they are running out of options.

Land of the Forgotten

The Senegalese government does not extend services to these people, even if they are in crisis. They are illiterate people who aren't counted in the census and do not even have the option to vote. Yet they have great resilience of spirit and know that something beyond their present thinking and abilities must happen if they are to survive the next dry season.

The group forms a circle to discuss the situation. As conservative Muslims, the men do all the talking. The women are not in the primary circle but sit at a distance in their own circle listening, but they do not speak.

In a moment of inspiration, feeling the power in the women behind her, Lynne senses that the answer to the problem rests in these quiet but powerful women. Then she does something very bold. She asks if she can visit with the women alone, knowing that only the chief and the mullahs are designated speakers for the tribe.

Possibly because of their desperate situation, they permit it and even allow their translator, a man, to join the women to translate for the delegation. Now, given their own voice, several women assume the leadership role and speak up immediately. They explain that they know there is a lake deep under the ground beneath them. They say that they can feel it; they are certain it is there. They explained that they had seen it in visions.

Their desire is not to have the delegation dig for the water; they ask only for their help in convincing the men to allow them to dig for it. They had previously explained to their men they knew how to find water; but having little voice and little credibility, the men did not believe them. Besides, women in this culture are not allowed to plan and dig wells; their job is weaving and desert farming.

The Muslim women's request seems small, but in context, it is huge. They are asking the men to do the unimaginable, to go against their deeply embedded cultural heritage, to step out of the box of their own limitations. Could they do it? Would they do it? Would this Hunger delegation lose their credibility by even suggesting it? And even if the men allowed it—what if the women didn't find water? There's risk involved here for everyone. Yet the women speak with such convincing certainty, the delegation is convinced these women can be trusted to find the water.

As Lynne ponders the women's proposal, she is overcome with the strength of the spirit of these women. In the midst of thousands of flies, with silt in her mouth and lungs, she feels no discomfort, only the presence of the spiritual strength of these remarkable women.

She remembers her thoughts about the expedition when it was in the planning stages: She had expected to find starving, hopeless, sick, poor people who expected this little delegation to do all the giving. Instead, she found them to be the gift. They had given her a new perspective—poverty is a state of mind, not a condition. These people are not poor; they are rich in spirit. They do not assume the role of victims; they are eager to face their challenge with perfect certainty they can accomplish the task with minimal help from our outside sources.

The Women...

Get permission from the chief and mullahs to dig the well with the understanding that the women could begin the project in partnership with their delegation. Often it takes a crisis before people will step out of their limited thinking and wake up to new possibilities.

Over the next year, the community rationed their existing supply of water. Then they began the project using hand tools and some simple equipment provided by the Hunger Project delegation. In an inspirational manner, the project begins with drumming and singing. Once the work begins, the women take turns caring for the children while other women dig and dig and dig, never doubting they will find water. The men watch with some skepticism, but allow the work to continue. The women are certain if they dig deep enough they will find water—and they do, just as they had seen it in their visions.

Because of this success, women gained new credibility. Men and women began working together to build a pumping system and a water tower for storage. Now not only does this little village have water, but sixteen other villages do as well. Because of the vision of a small group of inspired women, and the courage of the men to think differently, the whole region is transformed.

There are now women's leadership groups in all seventeen villages. There are literacy classes, batiking businesses, chicken farming and irrigation. All are becoming contributing members of their communities, and the communities are flourishing. The women are now a respected part of the community and have greater leadership opportunities.

This beautiful story gives us other clues about how to move from our confused world of 1% thinking to our peaceful, productive world of 99% thinking. It often takes stepping out of our self-limiting boxes and being willing to do something different. How many of us hang onto tradition as a kind of security blanket when it is no longer working? This is exactly what the desert people had done. If they had continued to disregard the women, they would have perished.

Yet we must appreciate what a huge move this was for the Muslim men to challenge centuries of tradition and allow women a voice. Because they had the courage to step out of tradition, a whole new power was unleashed to solve their problems, the power of inspired women. Stepping out of tradition was their biggest challenge, and they had the courage to do it.

Will we exhibit the same courage? In our modern society, we have a thousand confused 1% voices shouting at us every minute. They shout at us through the TV, the movies, the radio, and the Internet. They shout through our houses, our cars, and all the other stuff that demands our constant care and attention.

How can we find room for that quiet yet powerful inner 99% voice to filter through all the chaos? Meditation is one effective tool to reconnect to that voice.

So is spending time in nature, pondering what nature has to teach. Another is doing mindless chores, like chopping vegetables, ironing, or yard work. Taking a shower is another tool. These activities put minimal demands on the mind, allowing a space to let in that still small voice.

Two objects can't occupy the same place at the same time. Likewise, 1% and 99% thinking can't occupy our mind at the same time. We must choose.

The Senegalese, undistracted by a chaotic society, living in nature's desert, are in tune with their inner world. When facing a life-threatening situation, survival forces them to break out of tradition and break out of a dysfunctional paradigm regarding the roles of men and women, which had kept them imprisoned in mediocrity. After breaking out of a dysfunctional tradition, they were able to engage the inner powers of their women. Seventeen villages are then raised to a higher level of function and all become prosperous. Breaking out of dysfunctional traditions is also an ingredient in your recipe for prosperity.

Appreciate your adversity. When your adversity reveals that no other options out there work, a miracle takes place. A new desire is born, a desire to find your inner guru who can solve all problems and create the life you truly desire.

Adversity is a catalyst for getting in tune with the real you.

Challenge your dysfunctional thinking and traditions that hold you back.

Get your inspiration—*and get to work.*

As the Hunger Project delegation packed up to return home, they left in awe of what they had witnessed and remembered the wise words that came from the ancients:

"If you come to help me, you are wasting your time, but if you are coming because your liberation is bound up with mine, then let us work together."

They did work together—men and women, Americans and Senegalese. And everyone involved was lifted, for a time, from this dark, dense world of ego to a higher place.

For me personally, this story of the Muslim women confronted me with an old tradition I still hung on to that certainly hadn't worked for me. I, like these women, had allowed men to do my thinking for me. Was it because I was trained that way, or was it, in part, because it was just easier not to take the responsibility?

Our ascent from 1% to 99% thinking requires we ask and answer the hard questions.

Chapter Fifteen

THE RUSSIAN WHO SAVED AMERICA

Do you not see that all misery comes from the
strange belief that you are powerless?
— From *A Course in Miracles*

This story is about an unsung hero, a man whose heroism would have been unnecessary had our country, and his, not been trapped by fear. We felt so powerless that we built weapons of mass destruction to protect us against the Soviet Union. Meanwhile, the Soviet Union was doing the same thing…and in an event few ever heard about, they came within seconds of destroying the world, as we know it. In the following story, you will find how living by this erroneous 1% thought nearly cost us our lives.

What causes such feelings of powerlessness? Living a 1% life? Yet that is all we can live until we do the work necessary to find our real selves in our 99% world. Until then, we still need our heroes. Our heroes show themselves when, at least for a moment, they tap into their 99% powers and do something extraordinary. Such is the case with USSR Lt. Col. Stanislav Petrov. Because of him, we in America, and millions of others, are alive today.

A little background on Soviet/U.S. relationships can help us better appreciate the significance of Petrov's actions.

In 1983, the relationship between the United States and the Soviets was at low tide. The Reagan administration, fearful of trailing the Russians in the nuclear arms race, was afraid the Soviets might be tempted to launch a first strike on the United States. The Soviets had the same fear, that the United States might be tempted to launch a nuclear strike against them.

On September 1, Korean Airlines flight 007, a civilian airliner, entered Soviet airspace due to a navigational error. The plane was immediately shot down, killing all 269 passengers and crew. At first the Soviets denied any knowledge of the incident, then claimed the plane's intrusion was a deliberate provocation.

At the same time, NATO members were ramping up for a military exercise known as Able Archer, designed to prepare the U.S. nuclear forces in Europe for Soviet attack. Able Archer, spanning Western Europe, would be far more detailed and realistic than any previous exercise, which added fuel to Soviet paranoia.

This is where Lt. Col. Stanislav Petrov enters the picture.

Have you ever heard the name Col. Petrov? Few people have. His story is amazing and teaches us that there are many good people in all countries, even in those countries with whom we have ideological differences. It deserves to be more widely known, and so does he.

On September 26, a software glitch in Russia caused the USSR's early warning satellite to interpret sunlight bouncing off of the tops of clouds as five incoming American missiles. This triggered the Soviet response system, the first step in launching an attack on the United States. If the planned chain of events had taken place, every major city in the United States would have been eradicated, and the American military would have responded in kind. The world as we know it would have been destroyed, leaving nothing but a living hell for the survivors, who would have envied the dead.

What kept this nightmare from coming true?

Just one man: Lt. Col. Stanislav Petrov, who was in command of the unit that monitored the satellite. He had standing orders for this kind of situation; one push of a button would have set off a rapid cascade of events leading to nuclear attack on the United States. Yet Lt. Col. Petrov didn't sound the alarm. He felt a deep certainty that the computers were wrong, that this was not what it seemed, and it would be wrong to trigger a catastrophe in response.

By insisting the computers were wrong, he also showed us the monumental blessings that come from listening to the still small 99% voice inside, instead of heeding the fear of his colleagues who screamed in his ears from all directions. The fear exhibited by Col. Petrov's colleagues also screams in our ears from the voices around us.

Petrov's colleagues and superiors, living in fear, outfitted with mental blinders, would have let the attack go forward rather than risk being wrong. But Col. Petrov listened to love instead of fear. Because he did, you and your loved ones are now alive.

For his noble efforts, Petrov's superiors eventually forced him out of the military.

An Unacknowledged Hero

While the Russians have been reluctant to acknowledge Col. Petrov for his monumental courage—which saved their lives as well—in 2004, the World Citizens Association did honor his extraordinary contribution to humanity.

A professor named Metta Spencer, who was heavily involved in the peace movement and spent a lot of time in Russia, wanted to do something more to show her appreciation and gratitude. She started and donated to a monetary fund for his benefit. The money was to be transferred to Col. Petrov by a reliable friend in Moscow.

I contacted the professor to see if she was still looking for donations. She informed me that she hadn't heard from Col. Petrov for over five years and that he was a widower and had become an alcoholic, a common occurrence in Russia. The last she heard he was living in an apartment building without any hot water—a sad ending for such a hero, who for one critical moment listened to his inner voice, the voice of love, and saved the world.

Petrov's life also teaches us that if we don't continually work to find and stay in touch with the 99% world, the default voice of our 1% world will take over.

Because he became an alcoholic, we can deduce that he lost touch with that inner voice and allowed the much louder voice, the voice of fear, to dominate.

Still sadder than Col. Petrov's fate is the fact that we have learned so little from our "near death" experience. How long will it take and how much blood will have to be shed before we are ready to say, "What we have been doing is not working to create peace. What can we do differently?"

Peace can only be found in the 99% world. To try to find it elsewhere is to search for it where it cannot be found. War is always fear-based, a way to solve problems where they cannot be solved.

Chapter Sixteen

THE THRIFT STORE JACKET

*You can't have a perfect day without doing something
for someone who'll never be able to repay you.*
—**John Wooden**, UCLA basketball coach

It's hard to believe that a $3, secondhand jacket could change anyone's life, but it changed mine. It all began with a trip to a forgotten world hidden deep in a canyon in the Sierra Madre Mountains of Central Mexico.

I Remember the Terror...

... of the flight. Sitting on a hard wooden crate, I listened to the old freight plane rattle and groan. Hearing what sounded like loose bolts banging against the body, I expected the wings to fall off and crash to the earth at any moment with me a short distance behind.

"Dear God," I prayed, "if I have to die, please let it be fast and don't let it hurt." Miraculously, we landed on a short, rough dirt runway in San Andreas, a Huichol village just above Los Guayabos, our destination. I've never been sure the pilot made it safely back to Tepic.

I'd learned of the distress of the Los Guayabos tribe from a local newspaper while taking an extended vacation to Nuevo Vallarta. Rita Burns, a local artist, had been trying to help by selling her paintings. It wasn't enough. Rita was desperate for help. I responded, and this trip was the result.

Our mission: to visit the Los Guayabos tribe deep in the canyon and assess their needs.

Knowing we'd need help carrying our supplies down the treacherous mountain, we used sign language, broken Spanish, and several items of clothing  to bargain with the San Andreans. It was a pair of Levis that ultimately got us the loan of a burro. Several hours and a few spills later, we arrived bruised and exhausted, bearing gifts: a fifteen-pound papaya and two sacks of clothing, which included the thrift store jacket.

It was late when we arrived, but our hosts fed us a dinner of delicious corn tortillas and beans cooked in a tiny dark kitchen on the community stove.

After dinner, an elder motioned us to follow. After walking about 50 yards, he stopped at a tiny bamboo hut sitting on stilts. We'd be sleeping in the community pantry, which reminded me of a cage.

Exhausted as we were, we slept on the wavy bed of bamboo only a few hours before we were awakened by itching from the rough wool blankets and what felt like fleabites from the blankets' inhabitants.

Part of the Rock
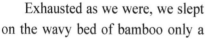

The next morning Mike, one of my traveling companions, approached the tribe's shaman. Mike had visited the village before and knew the shaman, and soon he'd talked him out of some peyote. We were about to witness something we'd never seen before.

I watched, fascinated, as Mike began peeling the peyote. "My fingers are going numb!" he said with both excitement and trepidation.

I wondered what it would do to his brain if simply peeling it caused his fingers to go numb, but he'd invited no response from us. We sat silently and watched and listened.

Next Mike cut off a chunk of peyote, put it in his mouth and began to chew. We watched closely, waiting to see if he could keep it down, ready to quickly pull him towards the door of the bamboo hut and make certain his head was outside the door if he was going to upchuck.

Mike squirmed. "I'm feeling nauseous."

Just as we're ready to lunge forward and pull him towards the door, his left hand popped up from the elbow like a stop sign on the side of a bus, and he said, "Wait, I think I can keep it down!"

We watched him close his eyes and calm himself as if drawing on higher resources to help. Finally, his body relaxed; he was in control and we relaxed as well.

When he opened his eyes, he said, "I need some fresh air." We helped him down the bamboo ladder and walked him to a huge flat rock, large enough for us all to sit comfortably. There Mike moved through a hallucinogenic experience, continuing to explain his sensations.

The rock had absorbed the warmth of the sun and radiated it back, so the same gentle sun warmed both our backs and our souls as he shared his experience. What I remember best is Mike explaining that he felt like part of the rock, and I get a glimpse into why the Huichols might use it in religious ceremonies. Eastern religions speak often of our oneness with all that is, and Christ told his disciples that he wished they could be one as he and his father in heaven were one. Clearly, oneness is an important spiritual theme.

The Tribal Meeting

Before we met with the tribal elders, we distributed the clothing we'd brought. Among the clothing was a jacket I'd bought at a thrift store for my son who kept losing his expensive stylish jackets. I'd warned him that if he lost another jacket, his next one would come from a thrift store. He lost another jacket and I bought him this thrift store jacket, as promised. He refused to wear it. It pained me every day he walked out the door in freezing weather without a coat, but he needed to learn the hard lessons of being responsible, so I endured the pain. He survived the winter without a problem, better than I did.

Having had little wear, the coat was like new. Still, to me, it was just a cheap jacket. It was about to be transformed into a miracle.

Going through the bag of clothing, one elder spotted the coat. His eyes lit up and his huge grin revealed several missing teeth. He carefully lifted the jacket from the bag and held it out in front of him with two thin arms and weatherworn hands. He looked at it for a very long time. Then he slowly pulled it to his chest and hugged it as if he were holding a miracle, an answer to his prayers. At last he slipped on the jacket.

"Oh, no the sleeves are too short," I thought as my body tensed. He didn't seem to notice. Style meant nothing; perfect fit was a luxury he didn't expect. He was simply full of gratitude for the gift of warmth.

Tears filled my eyes as I witnessed true humility and genuine gratitude for this jacket, which had cost me all of $3. An image of my own overstuffed closets flashed behind my eyes. I realized that in my spoiled society, we'd never done without. Humility and gratitude were only words we'd read in Scripture. I closed my eyes and reflected on the value of struggle and lack in the development of a humble soul.

I don't know how the others responded to the remainder of the clothing; I was focused on the drama of the coat. After all the clothes had been distributed, we began our meeting.

We learned that contaminated, bacteria-filled water was responsible for killing one-third of their babies. They needed our help in obtaining a clean water supply. When we returned to the United States, we wrote a proposal soliciting help from CHOICE (Center for Humanitarian Outreach and Intercultural Exchange), a humanitarian organization dedicated to connecting with motivated villages to provide resources and tools to change their lives. With their help and our combined networking ability, we provided the villagers at Los Guayabos a clean water supply, built them a tiny hospital and supplied them with eyeglasses to help them with their intricate beadwork. These were our gifts to them. Their gift to us was even greater. They'd helped us to see that for too long, we'd forgotten the most important things in life, like serving our less fortunate brothers and sisters. We'd failed to notice them because we were shopping.

As we left the village to begin our ascent up the mountain, about a half mile ahead we saw a mother walking, barefooted, with her baby curled hammock-style in her apron, lying so very still . . .

I said a silent prayer for all of us: that she would stay healthy, that her baby would survive, and that I would never forget the lessons of the thrift store jacket and the tiny, still baby wrapped in its mother's apron.

I sought my soul,
But my soul I could not see
I sought my God,
But God eluded me
I sought my brother,
And I found all three.
—Anonymous

Being a giver is another major key in being able to open the door to finding our real selves the in the 99% world we're seeking.

You will not see the light until you give it to others.
— From *A Course in Miracles*

Artist, Utahns join hands to help tribe in Mexico

20 CHOICE volunteers will travel to remote village to help Huichols.

By Alan Edwards
Deseret News staff writer

In a mountain range in central Mexico, 144 Huichol Indians in the remote village of Las Guayabas scrape at the soil, sleep on the floors of bamboo huts and worship various gods in their thatch-roofed temple.

"Their lives haven't changed in 500 years," said Claudia Goates, executive director of the International Association for Families in Salt Lake City.

Extremely poor and without clean water, the Huichols have a 30 percent mortality rate from infection and dysentery. They sell their native artwork in the cities to supplement their meager food and clothing supplies.

Four years ago, Rita Zanoni Burns, an artist from San Diego living in Puerto Vallarta, befriended the Huichols of Las Guayabas. She sold their artwork, gave them money and earned their trust.

Burns became enamored of the Huichols' original paintings, yarn pictures and carvings covered with multicolored beads.

"The Huichols are truly ancient artists," Burns said. "They've been doing it for 500 years."

Burns grew so fond of the Huichols and did so much to improve their lot that the head shaman of Las Guayabas began calling

her "mama." A Mexican newspaper labeled her "artista de la vida" — artist of life.

But Burns had a problem. Cataracts had stolen much of her vision, and she did not have enough money for an operation.

Enter Claudia Goates.

Goates recently found out about Burns' efforts and problems and began pulling strings. As a result, in June Burns found herself at Cottonwood Hospital in Murray, cataract-free thanks to Dr. George Pingree. At no cost.

"That was the first miracle," Burns said.

The second miracle was a meeting with the Center for Humanitarian Outreach & Inter-Cultural Exchange (CHOICE), a nonprofit charitable organization. After hearing Burns' account of conditions in Las Guayabas, CHOICE agreed to help.

In December, 20 CHOICE volunteers will travel to Las Guayabas to build a road to the village, dig wells to provide a clean water supply and teach the villagers about agricultural methods. They will give the villagers food and clothing, and doctors will provide them with eyeglasses.

"They don't have much in the way of agriculture," Goates said. "Food is a real big problem for them." She said Las Guayabas natives subsist primarily on rice, beans and tortillas ground from their corn crop.

Just getting the volunteers to Las Guayabas will be a challenge. The route to the village includes flying to Puerto Vallarta, riding a

Rita Zanoni Burns and Claudia Goates display an intricate beadwork mask made by the Huichol Indians, who live in central Mexico.

bus 150 miles to Tepic, taking a bush plane to San Andres and hiking three hours down a steep canyon wall to Las Guayabas. It is on that wall that the volunteers will hack out a road.

"It's like hiking to the bottom of the Grand Canyon," Goates said.

A little help goes a long way for the Huichols.

"They don't know about anything, so they don't know what to ask for," Goates said. "So what they ask for is minimal."

The Huichols' reaction to a $3 jacket from Deseret Industries was typical.

"It was like you'd given them solid gold, they were so happy," Goates said.

Chapter Seventeen

ANNA'S STORY

This is the world of opposites. And you must choose between them every instant...yet you must learn alternatives for choice, or you will not be able to attain your freedom. Let it then be clear to you exactly what forgiveness means to you, and learn what it should be to set you free.
—From *A Song of Prayer*, supplement to *A Course in Miracles*

Anna's story is drama at its best, beginning with the setting in which it took place. Sometimes stories come when you least expect them. I'd been invited to a gathering of women, an amazing group of women, all with psychic healing powers. Each marched to her own amazing drum. The opinions of others are of no concern to them; they know who they are and what they came to this planet to accomplish. I know I'm in for...

An Interesting Evening

I'm not disappointed. The meeting is at Sandra's. Sandra doesn't answer the door; she expects us to walk in. When she appears, she's dressed in her silky lime-green pajamas with black swirly designs, and her feet are covered with fuzzy bunny slippers. I wonder about the Hawaiian-style shirt she wears over her pajamas. I don't have to ask. Sandra, being telepathic, reads my thoughts and responds.

"This is a very expensive shirt," she smiles as she speaks. "It belonged to a good friend who died and left me all his shirts. I feel close to him when I wear it."

In this group, it's always something interesting. There's no agenda. We talk, eat and wait until our intuitive abilities set the flow in motion. Then we intuitively begin to split into groups and our stories begin about our experiences in the 99% world. Anna joins our group. In the middle of the stories we experience an unexpected surprise.

Jeff, Sandra's husband, comes home drunk...*really* drunk.

"We're from the FBI; we're investigating streakers in the area," Jeff slurs as he staggers through the door.

His boss, who is also drunk, parrots his story. "We're investigating some streakers in the area."

Deciding to go along with the game, I respond, "Cool, when you find them, can we take a peek?"

"Shuuur," Jeff says.

"Shuuur," comes the echo from his boss, who dwarfs him by eight inches.

Our friend Doris being a natural warrior bristles. "Get out of here Jeff, go to bed, you're ruining the spirit here!"

Jeff looks at her and says, "Ahh, don't be that way."

Sandra, his wife, appears from nowhere, takes Jeff's hand, looks at me and says lovingly, "They're so compliant when they're like this."

As she leads him slowly and gently around the corner and down the hall towards the bedroom, just out of sight, Jeff leaves us with his last entertaining words, "I want to have sex with somebody."

It is surprising that this would be the setting in which some incredibly spiritual happenings were about to take place; it's not the kind of environment one would expect to have a spiritual experience. The old me would have been disgusted with Jeff. I'd have left the party, and I would have missed the awaiting gift.

Fortunately, on this day I wasn't into judgments and chuckled to myself, "Ahh, total transparency; it's so refreshing." When Sandra returned to the living room I'm thinking, "This is better than a movie." Sandra looks at me and says, "You're thinking this is better than a movie, aren't you?"

I start to laugh, "No private thoughts in this place, I see."

You couldn't be inauthentic in this environment even if you wanted to. That's what I loved most about the group, their authenticity.

Before Jeff and the entertainment arrived and then disappeared, Doris had shared an amazing story that revolved around the purchase of a dry, old service-station candy bar that led to a conversation with the storeowner, which led to a spiritual experience. When she finished her story, I shared my "Old Radio" story. Eventually, the ladies begin to leave, leaving only Sandra, Doris, Anna and myself talking in the living room.

After a time, Sandra says, "I'm tired, I'm going to bed. You can stay and talk as long as you like."

We stayed—and talked. About midnight, Anna began speaking right in the middle of someone else's sentence. It was as if she had been programmed to begin telling her story at that moment and someone had just pushed the ON button and set her in motion.

Anna's willingness to be so candidly open with someone she'd just met amazed me. She later told me that it also amazed her. Her story is inspiring. It's nothing short of miraculous and I feel compelled to share it.

It's a story that demonstrates another way one can be reduced to ashes—besides a Ponzi scheme—and recover. It's an intimate and powerful story of how infidelity threatens to collapse a marriage, until Anna transformed everything in eight days by stepping into her 99% world of thinking.

When one person is able to step out of that confused 1% survival thinking, they can transform a pending disaster into a miracle. Anna is such a person.

Anna's Story as Told to Me

Eric, Anna's husband, had an affair with Kay. He'd been laid off from his high-paying job. No job, no money, no self-esteem is the cycle. But Eric had other things bothering him. What could better bolster a hurting man's self-esteem than to have a voluptuous woman desire him? While affairs are not uncommon it is uncommon to resolve it happily in only eight days.

Anna explained that Eric's affair began with what seemed to be an innocent friendship, with their children and Kay's children playing together. But Anna's deeply intuitive mind sensed that Kay had designs on Eric. Worse yet, it sensed that he, too, was interested in her. So, she invited Eric to sit with her in their comfortable posh living room chairs while they talked.

She got right to the point and asked…"Eric, are you interested in Kay?"

"No," he lied.

Over the next few days, his behavior would indicate that he hadn't been truthful about his feelings, so she asked again, "Are you attracted to Kay?"

This time he was truthful and said, "Yeah."

Her response was something I'd never have anticipated. She asked, "Eric, do you want to experience her?"

His response was equally unanticipated by Anna. "Yes," he said. "And I want a divorce."

Over the next week, Eric went back and forth between Anna and Kay, obviously torn. While Anna tried not to judge or condemn, she went through a tremendous range of emotions. She felt hope and connection when he said he was giving up Kay, followed by anger, sobbing and disconnection when he broke his word. She felt outraged that she'd just been wronged. She blamed herself and thought, "I'm the one who screwed up."

Her spiritual path had taught her to take full responsibility and not blame or judge—a remarkable and difficult demand in her circumstance. Her spiritual friends supported and reinforced that view and when she shared her story with

Sandra, she listened to her pain with no judgment and suggested she look for the growth lessons, keep positive, stay out of judgments and *look for the good!*

Anna knew Sandra was right and on the way home from her friend's house she was suddenly overwhelmed with gratitude for Kay. She realized she'd been a real gift and had taught her so much.

"I'd quit appreciating the blessings in my life. Having Kay come into our lives made me wake up and recognize the blessing I had. Someone had to show me how to be grateful," Anna explained.

On the way home, she drives into Kay's driveway, boldly walks up the sidewalk to the door and rings her doorbell. Kay answers the door and is startled to see her.

Anna gently touched her arm and sincerely said, "Kay, I am overwhelmed with gratitude for you. You're such a beautiful person and I hope your life will be filled with beauty and love. I really do love you! You've taught me so much!"

Kay responded misty-eyed. "I love you too! Thanks so much for coming; I needed to hear that."

When Eric came home that night, she asked Eric another surprising question: "Do you want me to fight for you?"

Eric, still living in his confused 1% world, responded, "I don't know!"

If she didn't know what he wanted— and he didn't know what he wanted, clearly she needed a wiser resource. That's when she asked God what she should do. She said she heard these words, "Let go and send them love, joy and blessings."

She did let go and felt a deep sense of freedom. But, again, her confused default thinking, stimulated by her 1% mind, took over. She again went into judgment and began hurting and got angry and confused again. To clear her mind she went for a drive and ended up at the bar where Kay worked. She sat down and began to cry. Kay was there. She saw Anna crying, walked over to her table and began gently rubbing her back to comfort her. Anna just let go and let her know how much pain she was in and how hard all this was on the children. She shared her worst angers and fears. As she did, they began bonding. They felt each other's pain as Eric had jerked them both around emotionally while trying to decide which of them he wanted. Kay thanked Anna for all the kind things she'd said to her when she went to her house and told her what an amazing woman she was.

"I think my words to Kay made her look at herself differently, as a better person than she or her reputation had branded her and gave her a vision for a better way," Anna explained.

As they are sharing, Anna's cell phone rings. It's Eric. Still angry, she tells Eric she doesn't have time to talk with him because she is with Kay at the bar.

I can't imagine what must have been going through his mind! Probably sheer terror that their conversations might reveal that he has not been totally honest with either of them. Suddenly Anna looks towards the entrance to the bar and is shocked to see Eric walk through the door and come towards them.

He pulls up a chair and joins them.

Anna looks Eric straight in the eye and asks, "What do you want?"

Kay chimes in and says, "Eric, you tell her the truth."

Anna supports Kay, "Yes, Eric, you tell us both the truth; we've been honest with each other, now it's your turn to be honest."

This is more than Eric expected. He'd underestimated his women! He knows the game is up. He is furious and no doubt terrified. It was no longer he and one of his women against the other; it is now his two women against him. He pops out of his chair and immediately stomps out of the bar.

When Eric got home that evening Anna was already in bed. (Who knows where he'd been for hours…probably trying to figure a way out of the corner his women had painted him into.) He's been humbled. He goes into the bedroom and lies gently beside Anna.

Still angry, Anna responds, "Sometimes I hate you, especially when I see the children hurting, and I don't know how to forgive you."

Then she gets up and goes into the other room and prays. "God I don't know how to forgive, but I'm *willing* to forgive…I need your help!"

Anna told us that at that moment, she knew: "It is finished. Immediately I'm able to forgive!"

From experience, I can tell you that this kind of forgiveness, originating in your 99% mind, is a mysterious process that can't really be explained. It can only be experienced with the help of divine intervention. It is powerful. It is real.

Anna goes back into the bedroom and asks Eric if they could talk some more. Things have been tense up to this moment. But tonight she can forgive it all and tells Eric, with the deep authenticity and sincerity, *that all is forgiven.* She tells him the experience she had with God when she left to go into the other room only moments before.

Eric starts to cry and says, "I'm so remorseful. I'm so sorry I've hurt you and the children. Please forgive me. You are the person I truly love."

His apology moved through Anna's whole being, for she knew it came from a place of deep and sincere love. "At that moment I knew that he couldn't ask for my forgiveness until he knew I was willing to forgive," she told us. "We have the most incredible physical relationship, better than we've ever had. It's ecstasy for both of us. We've never been more in love. I've learned that you can't be open at a physical level until you're open at an emotional level."

It's 1 a.m. as Anna finishes her story. Her cell phone rings; it's Eric.

After Anna hangs up she shares the conversation. Eric was about to go to bed but couldn't sleep until he knew she was okay and on her way home. He told her how much he loved and missed her.

On our end we heard her response, "I love you, too, darling and I am just leaving. I'll be home soon."

Reflecting

The conversation ended there and we all left for home, but the energy of the story stayed with me for days. I was amazed that they'd healed a troubled marriage in eight days. I compared it to my own marriage and traumatic divorce and tears pooled in my eyes.

The key was...true forgiveness. Their progress had been up and down for the week before that, but it couldn't hold. Nothing achieved in our confused world of 1% thinking can hold forever. True forgiveness takes place in our 99% world of thought where things achieved are permanent.

I continued to process all I'd heard and compare our experiences. At age fifteen, Anna had had her first child, whom Eric had adopted. They'd both struggled with alcohol and drugs. They'd broken many of society's rules. They'd gone through a lot, including what many would see as an unforgivable betrayal— yet their marriage was stronger than ever.

I'd lived my life as a conservative Christian obeying all the "right" rules, married to a physician, lived in a 10,000-square-foot house, raised an all-American family of eight children and strived for perfection. Perfection seemed a necessity to fit into my culture, so we faked it, hoping someday we'd really make it. It didn't happen.

Our marriage began as authentic, but after about seven years when our own repressed issues began to work their way to the surface for healing, we lacked the courage to face them. We falsely believed that it was the other's fault and things weren't right between us. That was something we couldn't face. We then had our children, so we began pretending everything was okay until the marriage dissolved into something inauthentic—plastic.

We didn't understand one important thing: *Problems in a marriage are quite normal.* Once you leave the honeymoon stage, you begin entering stage two of a healthy marriage, the healing stage. It's the stage when the relationship brings our unhealed issues out of the darkness of repression so our 99% mind can heal them. That's one blessing of a marriage: It can help us heal, freeing us to find our real selves.

If we fail to understand this, when problems appear, the relationship deteriorates into two egos using confused 1% thinking, in the battle to be right. This continually calls for making the other wrong. This, of course, never works.

Thinking with our 1% minds, we didn't understand that when stage two shows up it is really a valuable opportunity to heal buried issues that are trying to emerge for healing. We didn't understand that facing what appear to be marriage problems is really an opportunity to face our unresolved issues that kept us limited, disempowered and separated from ourselves, each other and most important, our creator and our real selves. We didn't understand that stage two is designed to help us grow individually so that our marriage could mature into something more beautiful than even the honeymoon stage, the mature stage.

Plastic Has No Strength

We were afraid to face what Anna and Eric so bravely faced, using total self- honesty and forgiveness to move into their 99% world, heal the marriage and move closer to finding their real, powerful, peaceful selves. Our plastic, 1% marriage was weak and shattered under stress.

We were caught in a Stepford culture that understood too little of the 99% world but was consumed by outward perfection. We had faded right into the culture, so when this stage of our marriage emerged, rather than use it as our creator intended, we hid behind our plastic life in our eggshell culture. But when we encountered heavy stresses, like murder and more, which put pressure on the plastic marriage, it collapsed, for plastic has no strength.

I wondered how two sophisticated people could be so naïve. When I realized that GI-generation parents had raised us both, it began to make sense. That generation had to survive the Great Depression, and then the war. They had developed a survival model for living: Just do your duty and don't complain. That became our model. We had no good models for authenticity.

Anna and Eric grew up in the Woodstock generation, which let it all hang out. Somewhere between GIs and baby boomers there is a happy medium, but here Anna and Eric provided me with a beautiful model of how authenticity triumphs over plastic perfection every time, if both parties are humbly working on it.

The power of Anna's story reverberated through my soul for weeks.

After trying to reduce all I'd learned from her story and mine to the lowest common denominator, I'd determined it boiled down to two things: being authentic and authentically forgiving. Yet never had I seen forgiveness more powerfully demonstrated. It's interesting to note that all Anna's efforts to stay out of judgment, and all Eric's resolve to go back to his family couldn't be maintained—until true forgiveness took place. Anna had to forgive Eric, and Eric had to forgive himself. Then it was done. The relationship was healed, just like that. So…

Let it then be clear to you exactly
What forgiveness means to you,
And learn what it should be to set you free.
—From *A Song of Prayer,* supplement to *A Course in Miracles*

Chapter Eighteen

OLD RADIO

THE VOICE

There is a voice inside of you
That whispers all day long,
"I feel that this is right for me,
I know that this is wrong."
No teacher, preacher, parent, friend
Or wise man can decide
What's right for you—just listen to
<u>*The voice that speaks inside of you.*</u>
— Shel Silverstein

But…make certain that your choice
Comes from your 99% voice.

It was my sister who said, "That radio is mine, and I'll steal it if I have to!"

It was my niece Kari who listened to that voice that spoke inside of her and saved her mother from herself—but that was only the beginning of the beauty Kari created by listening to that 99% voice inside of her.

Did my sister really plan on stealing the radio, if she had to? That's questionable. But her words are an indication of how desperately she wanted that old Zenith radio. When Barbara wanted something, she stopped at nothing until she had it. After our mother and sister were killed, she nearly singlehandedly got an amendment to the Utah Constitution changed to make laws tougher on criminals.

And this radio was much more than a radio to Barbara; it held precious memories. She'd been looking for that old radio for nearly five decades—a half-century!

Every few years Barbara would ask, "Mom, whatever happened to our old family radio?" And every time she asked, Mom's answer would always be the same; "I just can't remember!"

Mother's inability to recall what happened to the radio was understandable. At age forty-nine, a tragic automobile accident had claimed her husband, our father. The trauma of that loss, and the stress of being solely responsible for four fatherless children, and of making the decision to sell the family home left Mother's memories scattered.

Yet Barbara never forgot about that old family radio, and she prayed in her heart it would find its way back to its rightful home, *her* home. After decades of searching, Barbara quite unexpectedly ran into the old family radio—in the dusty corner of what had once been our garage.

Barbara had gone back to Ely, Nevada, for an all-class reunion in 2006. She decided to stop by the old family home and see if she could take photos for our family album. The new owners, Mr. and Mrs. A, were gracious and even offered to take her out to the large detached garage where, as kids, we used to sleep during the summer.

Memories flooded her mind as she walked through that old garage door. Upon entering the garage, Barbara's eyes were drawn to the corner where we kept the old cool can we would fill with punch for family picnics—a large, round grey-metal can with 2-inch walls and a 2-inch thick lid designed to keep our punch fresh and cold. Immediately an image of Brenda—dead in the cool can— pops up from her past. Two months after she had disappeared, we found Brenda, our cat, in the cool can, lifeless but perfectly preserved. She had gotten in our way while we'd been playing. Kaye and I asked Barbara to put her someplace where she wouldn't bother us. Then she *disappeared*. Barbara couldn't remember where she'd put Brenda!

Next Mrs. A. ushered Barbara to the old fruit room in the northwest corner of the garage. There was that old familiar knothole in the wall where the chipmunk I'd caught as kid bit my hand and escaped through the knothole into the space between the outer and inner walls. It, too, died in the garage.

Then Barbara saw it! Parked in a corner beneath decades of dust, old bottles, and bottle caps, looking very dead, sat the family radio—the 1945 Zenith radio to be specific, the one that had been missing for decades. Barbara's heart pounded in her chest, and she blinked twice to make sure it wasn't a mirage.

Observing Barbara's emotions and seemingly reading her mind, Mrs. A said, "Yes, this is your family's radio."

Barbara had long ago decided that if she ever found the radio, she'd pay up to $5,000 for it, although we later learned that it was worth much less, even at top price. While attempting to contain her excitement and sense of ownership, Barbara asked, "Would you consider selling that radio to me?"

Mrs. A's cordial demeanor abruptly soured. "Absolutely not," she said emphatically. "It belongs to my husband."

Barbara couldn't believe her ears. "I've searched for that radio for five decades. It's my radio; she has no right to it." The words went round and round in her mind, along with a few unprintable expletives she used to describe Mrs. A. "I'll get that radio no matter what it takes," she thought to herself. "I'll steal it if I have to—as a last resort, of course."

Barbara always got what she wanted, and by now her obsession with having this 1945 solid-walnut antique Zenith floor-model radio had become a bigger-than-life obsession because of the precious family memories it held for her. Barbara loved her family with an intense passion seldom rivaled. Having lost Dad at age forty-nine to a horrible automobile accident, and then Mom and Kaye to a brutal murder that occurred during a robbery, Barbara wanted desperately to hang on to every positive family memory she had—and for her that radio represented many positive memories.

Dad had owned a small Chrysler dealership in our little town of barely three thousand people. He advertised his business by radio—in Barbara's mind, on *that* radio.

Her older sister (that would be me) had entered a contest, which was broadcast over that old radio. I'd chosen to play "Malagueña," a difficult piano solo. Barbara had watched me practice, practice, and practice a difficult passage until my fingers bled, leaving blood smeared all up and down the keyboard. She never forgot those vivid memories of me preparing for that contest, and the even more vivid memories of being terrified I might not pull it off at the contest.

When the big day came for the contest to be broadcast, Barbara braced herself. Wrapping herself in an afghan Granny had crocheted, Barbara lay on the floor in front of that old radio. With the afghan tucked tight around her body, it seemed as though Barbara was protecting herself from what *might* happen.

When they announced that Claudia Tidwell would now play "Malagueña," Barbara, with clenched fists, yanked the afghan up around her neck and held it tightly there. When I got to the critical passage, she yanked the afghan over her ears and squeezed her eyes shut as if she were afraid to hear or see what might happen next—that maybe I wouldn't get through the passage without making a mistake. When I aced it, Barbara threw off the afghan and began turning cartwheels all around the room.

Barbara recalled the story of the sugar ration stamps, the ones I pasted on the back of that old radio. After all, what do you do with stamps? You paste them on something. But to my little five-year-old mind, they didn't look like they went on an envelope, and apparently I determined that the radio would do. Our mother simply had no appreciation for my five-year-old logic. All she could focus on was the fact that we wouldn't have any sugar for the rest of the month. I got a king-sized whopping.

For Barbara, all those memories—and more—were interwoven into the seams of that radio. She had to have it. She *would* have it. She'd try working through her friend, Pat Christiansen, who still lived across the street from our old house and who knew Mrs. A. well. She'd have Pat go talk to her. Pat tried, but to no avail.

She knew one of Mr. A's friends. She'd try to get him to buy it, and then she'd buy it from him. That didn't work either. That's when she told her children about the radio, and said, "If I have to, I will steal it!"

Enter Kari...

Barbara's only daughter.

Kari contemplated her mother's words. They stunned her a bit. Her mom had been raised with the Judeo-Christian principles, including "Thou shalt not steal," and had taught them to her children. While she couldn't believe that her mother would actually steal the radio, the fact she'd even considered it mortified her. Kari worshipped her mother.

While driving off the Kaysville freeway exit ramp, Kari received the revelation. She knew she had to get that old family radio for her mother for Christmas. Where would she start? She couldn't ask her mother for the people's name and address. She remembered their last name started with *A,* and that they lived on "G" Avenue in Ely, Nevada. From there she found their phone number.

Unlike her mother, Kari is neither aggressive nor confrontational. It terrified her to call and ask the A's if they would consider selling the radio to her, especially after how emphatic and rude they'd been to Barbara.

Kari had been taught to pray and felt that now she needed prayer more than ever. She began praying that God would soften the hearts of the A's. Kari prayed hard. Then she felt impressed to stop praying for her own needs and to begin praying for the needs of the "A" family. She prayed fervently that they would be blessed in their every need. She prayed their children and relatives would be blessed in their every need. And this Kari did with sincerity. She prayed in a way she'd never prayed before.

Finally, Kari felt the courage to call. With trembling fingers, Kari dialed the number. Secretly she hoped she'd get an answering service, so she wouldn't have to speak to them directly.

"Hello," Mr. A answered the phone.

Kari began to breathe hard, but had her message memorized, so no one could detect her fear.

"Mr. A, this is Kari Hatch. My brothers and I are wondering if you would possibly consider selling our old family radio back to us. We'd like to get it for our mother for Christmas. We're all raising young families and don't have much money. We're hoping we can afford what you ask."

After the negative interaction her mother had experienced with Mrs. A., Kari was quite surprised and highly relieved that Mr. A. was actually civil.

"How much do you think it is worth?" he asked.

"I have no idea," Kari responded. "It's worth to us lies in its sentimental value."

"I'll tell you what," Mr. A. said, "you get on the Internet and do some research, then call me again with what you find.

After about a week of frustrating research, full of dead ends, Kari finally determined that a 1945 Zenith floor model made of solid walnut sold anywhere from $250 in poor condition to $3,000 in refinished condition. She called Mr. A. and recounted all the research she'd done to finally find the information, all the roadblocks she'd encountered, etc.

Obviously touched that Kari would go to such incredible efforts—with only the hope she *might* get this radio for her mother—when she finished the explanation of her journey through the Internet to find the information he'd requested, Mr. A said kindly, " When can you come and get the radio? You'll be able to afford it." Although he couldn't see her tears through the phone, I'm sure he felt them in her voice as she thanked him.

On their way to Ely to pick up the radio, Kari and her sister-in-law drove through a snowstorm, traveling only fifteen miles an hour. When they arrived, Mr. and Mrs. A came out of their house and greeted them like long-lost family, even inviting them to come in and eat a special meal they'd prepared.

After the meal, they moved to the living room where they all immediately bonded, as they discussed their lives and interests. The A's invited them both to bring their children back to Ely so they could take them on a special fishing trip, and Kari invited them to visit her family in Layton, Utah.

As they walked to the garage to get the radio ready to transport, Kari felt a bit overwhelmed. What had begun as a fearful and adversarial situation had turned into three wonderful gifts: a gift to Kari from the A's, a gift from Kari and her brothers to their Mom, and the gift of a priceless, budding friendship between Kari's family and the A's.

Wish Your Mom a Merry Christmas!

Before loading the old radio onto the truck, Kari pulled out her checkbook to pay for it. Mr. A. smiled kindly and said, "Just wish your mother a Merry Christmas."

Kari fought back the tears as she thanked them profusely for their kindness and placed her checkbook back into her purse. Still overcome by the beauty of the experience, she helped Mr. A. place the old radio in the truck.

A miracle had just taken place. Not only had she gotten the radio for her mother, she'd done so in a manner that allowed everyone to win. Despite Mrs, A's initial grumpiness, now she also felt good about turning over the radio to Kari. She felt overjoyed at being able to obtain it for her mother, all three were delighted about the wonderful new friendship that was developing between them, and Kari's brothers, who were going to share in the cost, were delighted to be participating. Best of all, they knew their mother would be ecstatic.

I heard the full story from Kari after she'd presented the radio to her mother. We were sitting in the intensive-care unit at Utah Valley Hospital, devastated over our cousin, Larry, whose story I told in Chapter 11. In an effort to dissipate some of our anxiety and lift our burdened spirits, I asked Kari to share the story of the old family radio.

As Kari spoke, she filled in the amazing details of the story we hadn't heard before. The details were new even to her mother. Kari explained that once she and her sister-in-law Charlene managed to get the old family radio home from Ely into Kari's garage, she faced two new challenges.

The first: Kari had absolutely no experience refinishing furniture. Could she do it well enough to please her mother? She did have one advantage: Her brother-in-law built custom cabinets and could teach her how to sand it properly and where to get the custom stain needed to restore it. The new stain she had custom made became known and sold as Old Radio.

Kari continued her story, "My next challenge was to get the job finished without my mother finding out before Christmas." Barbara was in the habit of frequently stopping by Kari's unannounced. "Mom also makes a game of trying to figure out what we're giving her for Christmas long before Christmas ever shows up. The weeks that followed were intense. I had to keep the garage door open while sanding and staining the radio. Every time I'd hear a car approaching I'd panic and run out into the driveway hoping not to see my mother's red Toyota Corolla."

Kari's husband, Brandon, had removed the internal workings of the radio in an effort to restore them. These were also hidden in the garage.

"We'd kept our secret until the day I invited my mother to dinner. I'd locked the door to the garage just in case she got curious. However, it wasn't what was in the garage that threatened to give me away—it was my hands. My mother looked at them and scolded me. 'You need to take better care of yourself! Why are your hands so rough and stained?' I told her, 'It's just life, Mom.'" Kari was fearful her mother might figure out why they were in such a condition and once again, sleuth out her Christmas present before Christmas. She didn't—much to Kari's relief. This year, the grand gift of all her gifts to her mother would be a surprise.

When Christmas morning arrived, the family sat in Kari's living room watching the family video they had made during the year, a tradition they looked forward to each year. But this year was different. One by one the family members disappeared until Barbara sat alone in the living room. Puzzled by this strange occurrence, she got up to see where they had all disappeared. She found them. When she walked through the garage door, in unison they shouted, "MERRY CHRISTMAS!" They all were gathered around the old family radio, now perfectly restored inside and out.

Barbara burst into tears. It was the first time they'd ever seen their mother cry. If you had to describe Barbara in one word it would be *tough*. The only time she shows intense emotion is when she gets angry. Even after losing her beloved husband to a stroke at age fifty-seven, she moved quite quickly through the first stages of grief straight to anger, a place she found most familiar.

I often wondered if Barbara's tough exterior and all the anger was a way she continued to protect her broken heart over all the losses: Dad to an automobile accident, Mom and our sister Kaye to murder, her beloved husband to a stroke, her best friend to cancer. If Barbara held you off with her anger and never let you come too close, it wouldn't hurt so badly to lose you. She had a capacity for a deeper love than almost anyone I know and it terrified her. While her charm made her many friends and her relatives adored her, she always found some reason to be mad or unavailable if you got too close, or if she began to get too attached.

Yet as Kari tells us her story, as we are still gathered to support our cousin, and his family in the intensive-care unit, I see Barbara do something I'd never seen before.

Kari sits in her chair with her long, flaming red curls pulled back in a pony tail through her baseball cap, and as she speaks, a tender look of admiration and intense love for her daughter comes over my sister's face, such as I've never seen before in all her sixty-three years of life.

Kari's eyes sparkle as she finishes her story. "It was such an amazing experience for me. It was the best Christmas I've ever had. It was everything I hoped and prayed it would be—and even more!"

Home Again

The old family radio had found its way home, to its rightful home, Barbara's home, via the amazing Kari. It now occupies a prominent place in Barbara's living room. For a long time, it wore a red velvet crown Barbara rented from the costume shop. Now it displays, under glass, a baseball signed by Sandy Koufax.

The old radio story is quickly becoming a touching, inspirational family legend. It stands as a monument to that eternal truth: It is more blessed to give than to receive. Sincere giving blesses both the giver and the receiver.

Kari allowed her 99% mind to do her thinking and she created a win-win situation for everyone. The A's were happy, for they had an opportunity to do something very gracious. Kari and her brothers were all happy to have such a wonderful gift for their mother. Barbara was thrilled beyond words with the gift. Kari said it was best Christmas she'd ever had.

The story is not only a treasured family story; it is an excellent example of the contrast between our two thought systems and what each creates.

Chapter Nineteen

LESSONS FROM OUR STORIES

"How does one become a butterfly," she asked pensively?
"You must want to fly so much you are
willing to give up being a caterpillar."
—**Trina Paulus**, *Hope for the Flowers*

What did we learn from each of the stories in this section that would help us move from the world of fear-based, ego-based thinking to the place we want to go?

"Money Is Like Water" shows how *not being addicted* to money is another step that allows you to connect to that world where we solve all our problems. For it is our subtle or not-so-subtle addictions, money being the most common, which help keep us disconnected from our real self and our 99% world of love and peace.

"Miracle in the Desert" shows that before we can enter through the 99% door, we must step out of the box in which our old thinking keeps us imprisoned. To do that, we must be willing to let go of old beliefs and traditions that no longer serve us.

"The Russian Who Saved America" shows the absurd, dangerous things we will do when under the influence of fear. It also shows that even when under the influence of love, that we must work to stay there or again be taken over by ego fears.

"The Thrift Store Jacket" shows another requirement for connecting to the 99% world. The requirement is…giving. Giving to the Huichols began a flow of blessings of self-understanding I never could have gotten any other way. *Giving* always comes before, and allows for, receiving.

"Anna's Story" shows us how she connected to that 99% world and was able to save her marriage in only eight days by refusing to judge the woman who tried to steal her husband and by offering genuine forgiveness to her husband.

"Old Radio" shows how the confused world of 1% thinking leads us to try to solve problems in a destructive way. Proactive behavior is a requirement for walking through the door that opens into the 99% world.

The story also shows the dramatic difference in the results obtained when listening to the 99% voice of inspiration and love, rather than the 1% voice of fear. This is the greatest of human challenges; when it happens, it is a miracle, one that creates more miracles.

Let's summarize the qualities that connect us to our 99% world, as shown in these stories:

- Giving
- Forgiving
- Non-judgmental
- Free of addictions
- Willing to give up old traditions and beliefs that no longer serve you.
- Willing to listen to the still small voice and follow its instructions.
- Willing to practice these skills that take you out of your 1% world

Now we leave this 99%, win-win world with a deeper understanding of what it takes to get there, and an understanding of why we want to be there. Next we'll enter the world of science and mysticism, where we'll find yet more perspectives on what it takes to move from the 1% world to the 99% world.

PLASTIC SURGERY FOR THE SOUL

Solutions for peace are never political, philosophical, or militaristic. Violence [judgment and blame] even when justified... [are] merely fighting darkness with more darkness. Solutions must be founded upon spiritual Light and the human soul.

—Rabbi Yehuda Berg

The true source of our suffering has been our timidity. We have been afraid to think...

—Founding father **John Adams**

INTRODUCTION

In the first two sections, we showed you two worlds and the thinking patterns that create each world. This knowledge allows you to avoid the 1% thinking and incorporate the 99% thinking patterns into your life. This section will give you more angles from which to view the subject of moving from the place where we create our problems to the place we solve them. Here we'll validate our principles with science and mysticism, which are beginning to find a joining place.

We call this section "Plastic Surgery for the Soul," not because the soul needs fixing—it is perfect. It's called such because the soul is waiting for you to tighten the wrinkles in our thinking and remove your bulging misperceptions, which stand as barriers between you and your soul. It longs to reconnect.

Chapter Twenty

A NEW LAYER OF SELF...
AN EVOLUTIONARY LEAP

The snake that cannot shed its skin perishes, so do the spirits who are
prevented from changing [or won't change] their opinions [perceptions].
—**Friedrich Nietzsche**, 19th century German philosopher

While nature's creatures have a natural ability to perform their own surgery when something needs to be replaced, whether it is new skin or a new leg, it is not so easy for humans; we generally need help. This chapter is designed to keep our growth and freedom from perishing by providing the tools that explain how to replace old, too tight, ideas that keep us limited and imprisoned, and need to be shed. By doing this we make an evolutionary leap towards freedom.

Sometimes the results of our old thinking can be sad; sometimes they can be funny as illustrated by a new bride.

The bride called her mother in tears. "Oh, Mother, I wanted so badly to fix John a nice dinner tonight. He loves meatloaf and I followed Grandma's recipe perfectly and it turned out terrible. What could I have done wrong?"

"Let's go over what you did step by step and together we'll fix it," the mother said, comforting her.

"Okay," the bride sniffled. "Well, it starts out, 'Take fifty cents worth of ground beef.' " (Are you chuckling yet?)

While blindly following someone else's thinking without rethinking the information for yourself can produce hilarious results as with the meatloaf—Nietzsche points out, staying stuck in old, distorted thinking patterns and too-small perceptions can also be lethal. Yet how often do we accept what we're told without question? When we do, it often prevents us from discovering a new powerful layer of self that lurks beneath our old "reality," our too-small ways of thinking that prevent us from seeing the real powerful, brilliant us.

Accepting new ideas is rarely easy. However, it is essential, unless we wish to strangle our own personal growth and eliminate miracles in our lives. We need to find the courage to choose new thoughts. This applies to all mature minds, even to scientists who are trying to discover new ideas.

Take Erwin Rudolf Josef Alexander Schrödinger, for example. He was an Austrian theoretical physicist whose most notable contribution was the Schrödinger equation, for which he received the Nobel Prize in 1933. Schrödinger's equation opened the door for the new science of quantum physics, which so challenged his former perceptions that he later denounced his own research, saying, "If I'd known what trouble this damned quantum wave would cause I never would have invented the equation that produced it."

Einstein also had problems accepting some of his own discoveries. His own theories supported the new field of quantum physics based on possibilities, as did Schrödinger's discoveries. Einstein died without ever resolving his old beliefs with his new discoveries.

Yet quantum physics has opened the door for man to discover his own potential. Strangely enough we are more afraid of our potential and our power than we are of being powerless, as expressed beautifully by Marianne Williamson. Here's another new thought to challenge your ego a bit.

Our Greatest Fear

Our deepest fear is not that we are inadequate.
Our deepest fear is that we are powerful beyond measure.
It is our light not our darkness that most frightens us.
We ask ourselves, who am I to be brilliant,
gorgeous, talented and fabulous?
Actually, who are you not to be?
You are a child of God.
Your playing small does not serve the world.
There's nothing enlightened about shrinking so that
other people won't feel insecure around you.
We were born to make manifest the glory of God that is within us.
It's not just in some of us; it's in everyone.
And as we let our own light shine, we unconsciously
give other people permission to do the same.
As we are liberated from our own fear,
our presence automatically liberates others.
—Marianne Williamson

It is our light, not our darkness, that most frightens us.

To choose new thoughts wisely requires that we are willing to observe old thoughts and beliefs without judgment, then notice if they work to bring us peace.

Let me warn you, however, that the very ideas that will free you and bring you peace may first threaten you or make you angry. It is only after you accept them that they can set you free and give you peace. Someone once said, "First the truth will piss you off, then it will set you free." Why? Because ego (the fear-based thought system) does not want you to see truth because once you do, it will lose its control over your life. The fearful ego will violently protest when you come across these new ideas.

We'll start out easy with a new idea that could threaten the ego but shouldn't cause too much fear. See how you do with it. Here's a new thought on belief.

A belief is only a thought we think over and over and over again until it becomes a belief. A belief has little to do with what is or isn't true.

While observing and evaluating your beliefs, keep in mind what a belief really is. If your ego resists a new idea that challenges beliefs you already hold, it's not because the idea is wrong; it is because the ego is scared, which makes you scared.

Every negative thought or feeling, when reduced to its lowest common denominator, is fear-based and therefore of the ego. Any belief that does not eventually bring peace comes from judgment and/or a lack of willingness to give up old ideas—all rising from the ego.

The following stories illustrate how employing healthy thinking patterns to alter beliefs can take you to your 99% world where the real you resides.

Surviving Auschwitz

Dr. Viktor Frankl in his classic book, *Man's Search for Meaning*, shares with us how choosing his thoughts helped him survive three horrendous years at Auschwitz, one of the worst of Hitler's prison camps. He says:

> *We who lived in concentration camps can remember the men who walked through the huts comforting others, giving way their last piece of bread. They may have been few in number, but they offer sufficient proof that everything can be taken from a man but one thing; the last of the human freedoms—to choose one's attitude in any given set of circumstances, to choose one's own way. And there are always choices to make. Every day, every hour, offered the opportunity to make a decision, a decision which determined whether you would or would not submit to those powers which threatened to rob you of your very self, your inner freedom, which determined whether or not you would become the plaything of circumstance, renouncing freedom and dignity to become molded into the form of the typical inmate.*

> *Even though conditions such as lack of sleep, insufficient food and various mental stresses may suggest that the inmates were bound to react in certain ways, in the final analysis it becomes clear that the sort*

of person the prisoner became was the result of an inner decision, and not the result of camp influences alone. Fundamentally, therefore, any man can, even under such circumstances decide what shall become of him—mentally and physically.

Being one who believes "if life hands you a minus (-) you should make it into a plus (+)," I decided long before the Ponzi scheme that I would not become a victim of any circumstance. I made that decision after the murder of my mother and sister in 1990. Instead I decided to do what I could to make communities safer for families and formed a 501 (c) 3 international non-profit corporation to accomplish this goal.

After running out of the inheritance money with which I supported the organization, I began funding it through a program I began in the courts to rehabilitate those charged with drunk driving and domestic abuse. The judge gave those in court a choice of paying a huge fine or using the money to go through our program. That program emphasized, among other powerful concepts, the power in choice. I used Dr. Frankl's experience as an example and had the participants read some of what he'd written about it.

A young man named Stephen was one of the first to go through the program. He had always been highly discouraged about his life. Not knowing how to cope in a healthy way, Stephen continually sabotaged his life with alcohol and drugs. Yet he finally found freedom when he learned he had choices and how exercising those choices wisely could change his life. Had he not done so, he would eventually have ended up in prison. But because he came to understand choice and how to use it wisely, it changed his life. We'll let him explain it in his own words.

Dear Claudia,

It's difficult to express my appreciation and feelings on paper about last weekend and my life since then.

On Friday, I had absolutely no idea of what to expect, and it turned into an awesome experience.

What I learned about myself, what I was doing to myself and where I was heading was scary. I was not being myself, rather acting as someone I perceived to be me.

This past week has been unreal. All I can think about is the ability I have in choosing for myself what will work in my life.

I used to get upset easily. Now when I am aggravated, I stop to think if this is how I want to act. People at work have asked me why I'm so happy. My best friend (which I have known for over 10 years) has noticed a change in me. I'm a better person than I have been the past couple of years.

Life is still difficult at times, but it's not drudgery anymore. It's amazing the perception that can be achieved about life when the perspective is from a different angle.

To be blunt, I feel damn good! I would recommend this experience to anyone. It sure lifted some dead weight off me.

Life is exciting again, and now I'm able to act on it.

Thank you very much!

Love, Stephen

There you have it. Almost seventy years ago a psychiatrist objectively observed his difficult circumstances and chose thinking patterns that created a miracle, helping him survive the worst of Hitler's Nazi prison camps.

Then, only a few years ago, Stephen did something similar: he observed his life, recognized it was spiraling downward fast, thought about it, chose to get into our program, which helped him think about life differently and make new choices. This created a miracle that turned his life around and kept him out of prison.

You can set yourself free from your own self-imposed prison by letting go of your old, too-tight thinking, which keeps you imprisoned in your 1% world of fear.

Summary of Sections 1 and 2, Preview of Section 3

Section One was written to show how our fear-based thoughts create a lose-lose world for everyone. *Any negative, judgmental thought or action, when reduced to its lowest common denominator comes from some form of fear and causes pain and suffering.*

Section Two was written to show the contrast between the two worlds. It shows how love-based, 99% thoughts and actions create a win-win world for everyone.

In Section Three, we're offering tools to help you escape your 1% world. They are tools you may already have in your toolbox of awakening. We are simply pointing to your tool of choice, encouraging you to sharpen it and use it more effectively and reminding you of its power to awaken you to who you really are.

You only have two choices:

- Continue living in this ego world of fear and pain, remaining confused, never finding the real powerful you.

- Remove the barriers that keep you stuck in fear so you can find your world of love, where the real and powerful you resides.

Which will you choose? Don't we all desire No. 2? Are you willing to do the necessary work?

Before you choose, let's look at some scientific evidence that supports the principle that our thought choices do create your world.

Motivational thinkers have been telling us for decades that what we think is what we get. Now science is telling us how it happens. It begins with observation—that is, becoming consciously aware of something.

Chapter Twenty-One

CREATING MIRACLES

You can't look at something without changing it.
How you look can determine the changes you experience.
—**Alan Wolf**, quantum physicist

The following is a visual image illustrating Dr. Wolf's quote.

Tilt your head to the right. What do you see? A word?

Now tilt your head to the left and what do you see? The profile of a man's face?

Life is a two-sided coin. After observing that one side is negative and the other positive, which side will you focus on? When you focus on one side, you eliminate the other. Are you going to view your life from the perspective of a victim who lives in fear, or of a victor who lives in love? The choice you make determines your future. When you get this at a gut level, as Stephen did, you've taken the first step on your path to freedom and empowerment. Here you'll see, from a scientific perspective, how

175

you can move from victim to victor, fear to love by using *observation, thought, and choice.*

Quantum physics is a relatively new science that has turned the traditional scientific world upside down because it puts the responsibility for how our lives turn out right back in our laps. This new physics came into prominence with the famous *wave particle experiment.* This experiment helps us understand, from a scientific point of view, what happens when we observe a situation and choose to take action. The choice we make determines our destiny. Quantum physics gives validity to the concept that *by changing our minds we can change our lives.* The following visual model will help make the physics easier to understand.

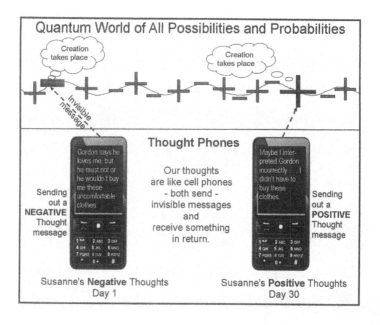

Here's how it works. Our thoughts are like cell phones; they both send out invisible messages that connect to something or someone out there. Once connected, something new is created.

There are *many possibilities that can* result from a cell phone, depending on the number you dial and the conversation you have. You are not always certain what possibility will be created; it can heavily depend on the person at the other end. You're not always in control.

There are *infinite possibilities and probabilities* that can result from your thought phone, depending on the thought you choose. By sending out a *chosen* thought, you, alone, determine the result your mind phone will bring. You are in total control.

At the quantum level, there is an energetic, quantum world where unlimited possibilities and probabilities for your life exist—the good, the bad, the ugly, and the beautiful.

Every thought you put out connects to a possibility in the quantum world that matches your thought. When the connection takes place, the result is manifest. Unlike the cell phone where the person at the other end can largely determine the result of the communication, your mind phone has total control.

*To connect to the possibility you want to manifest in your life, **you choose** the thoughts that will connect to the possibility you desire, which is found in the quantum world of all possibilities.*

Everything in the quantum world remains only a possibility until you connect to it with a thought, then a result manifests.

Everything when reduced to its lowest common denominator is wave energy, including you and your thoughts.

If you want peace, you continually think peaceful thoughts. It's a discipline. If you want abundance, think abundant thoughts. It always works…**unless** you have a dog sled condition discussed later in this chapter.

That is how you change your life. You change your thoughts. It's that simple.

Susanne and Gordon

The following story is true. It demonstrates how one woman changed her mind, her interpretation of the past, and by doing so—changed her future.

Remember this: *Everything, including your past, is only an interpretation of what you thought you saw and/or experienced.*

There's another thought to challenge your thinking.

Scenario One

Susanne had a generous boyfriend, Gordon, who enjoyed buying her beautiful clothes. He picked out a dress and coordinating shoes; when she tried them on, they weren't comfortable. But they were beautiful, so she said nothing and allowed him to buy the clothes.

Later she began thinking, "Although he says he loves me, he must not, or he wouldn't want to buy me these high heels that hurt my feet and that dress I can hardly breathe in. He just wants someone to make him look good."

This thought now became what she believed to be her past, because a past is simply *an interpretation* of what you think happened. By *changing your interpretation of what you think happened, you change your future*. In this case, Susanne's interpretation of her past created a not-so-pleasant future, one without a generous boyfriend whom she broke up with—without ever explaining why.

Scenario Two

In a new present moment, sometime later, Gordon called Susanne. By this time she missed him and had begun reconsidering her position. She thought, "Maybe I interpreted him incorrectly. Maybe he had no idea how uncomfortable these high, high heels would feel—after all, I doubt he's ever worn high heels. And I didn't have to let him buy them. I could have told him they were uncomfortable."

What just happened? By reinterpreting the shopping trip, she just *recreated her past*. Again, *all of our past is simply an interpretation, only our perception, of what happened.* This is one of the most valuable lessons we can learn.

When Susanne thought differently, she treated Gordon differently; because she treated him differently, he responded differently. Now they are seeing each other again and have become close friends. She *recreated her future* with her new thought, her new interpretation of the past.

Now you see how our thoughts create our past and determine our future! And from our model, you also see that many possible outcomes are available to us in any situation. What we see depends on how we choose to interpret or think about what happened.

How did I learn this lesson? It happened in 1991 in a tiny courthouse in Coalville, Utah, just east of Park City. Von Taylor and his partner, Edward Deli, were sitting in the courtroom in front of the judge dressed in orange prison jumpsuits with chains around their legs on trial for murdering my mother and sister.

The Red-leather Skirt

The last witness to testify was my niece Linae, who'd witnessed the murders. As she walked back from the witness stand, I could see her almost go into a trance, as if something inside were splitting. It startled and concerned me. When the jury began their deliberations and the family was guided into a small room to wait for the verdict, I knew I had to find a way to help her.

There weren't enough chairs in the room where we waited so I sat on the floor. I doodled on a piece of paper as I waited for my mind to produce a thought that would help Linea. Finally I had an idea. I turned to her and said, "When you begin to replay this tragedy, instead of seeing bullets coming out of the guns, see butterflies. Then watch them fly over to Grams and Kaye and see them light gently on their heads, putting them into a beautiful, peaceful sleep."

Years later, Linae told me she didn't remember what I'd said; she had been in shock and couldn't listen. When I asked her again later, she told me that it had all come back to her. My sister Barbara remembered and it really helped her. But she didn't remember the scene accurately. First, she thought my husband, a psychiatrist, had supplied the image, although he wasn't even there.

Sometime later we were discussing the trial and Barbara said, "I thought it was very strange the way you handled things at the hospital when we went to see Rolf. [This is Kaye's husband, who had been shot twice in the head, set on fire and left for dead]. You were just sitting in the corner in your red-leather skirt taking notes."

At first I was shocked, with no idea of what she was talking about.

As I thought about it, I realized she must have been thinking of the experience in the courthouse and had it mixed up with the hospital. When I tried to straighten things out, Barbara insisted that she was right—it had happened in the hospital and I was in the corner taking notes!

I thought, "Either she is very mixed up or I am!" I was also positive I was right. To make certain, I decided to call three other people who were there in that room and see what they remembered. Each person had a totally different version of what happened. And each was certain they were right! Granted, the more stress you are under, the more inaccurate your perception is likely to be. So the best way to communicate is to simply share our perceptions and recognize that's all they are.

It is a waste of time to play "I'm right, you're wrong" games. Instead, acknowledge that everything is perception, our interpretation of what happened. The best way to handle a potential "I'm right, you're wrong" conversation is to simply suggest you each share your perceptions, examine both, and work together to develop a more accurate, more holographic perception than either of you had before.

If all of us were capable of using our 99% thinking all the time, we would all have the same truth, or at least, the same perception. But that can't happen as long as we remain in the 1% world.

Now I'll describe an experiment that further explains *how* we create with our thoughts.

The Wave-Particle Experiment

Visualize a white movie screen. In front of that screen is a black screen with two slits placed close together. The black screen is off to the right a bit so some of the white screen is still exposed to let us know it's there. In front of the black screen, a little distance away, is a particle projector. This projector handles subatomic particles called free electrons, which are usually bound within an atom. The purpose of the experiment is to shoot free electrons through the slits on the black screen and see what kind of patterns they form on the white screen.

Scientists set things up, turned on the particle projector, then turned their backs and went on about their business while the experiment ran. When the machine had done its job, they turned to the white screen to analyze the patterns.

Much to their amazement, the particles didn't register on the white screen as if they were particles at all. Instead they appeared in a wave-interference pattern, meaning that the particles had suddenly become waves.

This astonished the scientists. They decided to do the experiment again, only this time they closed down one of the slits. Again they were astonished at the result. The pattern on the white screen could only have been made by particles. The wave had again become a particle.

Why, the scientists wondered, did this thing act like a wave when it went through two slits and a particle when it went through one slit?

Going Deeper

Finally they realized that this thing was *both* a wave and a particle. But what determined whether it showed up as a wave or as a particle?

THE BIG NEWS IS...it behaved as a particle when man interacted with it. Without man's interacting with the electron, it would have remained a packet of possibilities and probabilities. When the scientists closed down one slit, it limited the possibilities of how the electron could manifest. Introducing the second slit opened up the possibilities of both a wave and a particle.

What does this mean to us? It challenges us to ask a question about our own minds. Do we have a one-slit mind that allows for only one-way life can manifest, eliminating other possibilities? Or have we developed a two-slit mind, one that opens up the door to other possibilities?

*Until man observes something, thinks about it and **chooses** what he desires to manifest with it, everything, every situation, remains an undeveloped wave of possibility.*

Waves are simply energy that can take form in an infinite number of ways. So when we're studying quantum physics we're studying how the mind interacts with wave energy to manifest its infinite possibilities and probabilities.

Through his theory of relativity, Einstein showed us that matter can change into energy and back into matter, demonstrating they are just alternate expressions of the same thing. When our quantum-wave minds interact with the quantum-wave energy out there, we tell it how to manifest—as money, as a new relationship, or as poverty and no relationship, as Susanne discovered.

Traditional science has not yet found a satisfactory way to measure the quantum world of mind, for these quantum waves don't conform to the laws of mechanical motion, which operate in the 1% world of form. This means scientists must come up with a new set of tools for testing this 99% phenomenon. Yet for centuries, eastern religious philosophies and mystics have acknowledged, and taught, that man can indeed change his life by changing his thoughts.

Perhaps science will catch up with these older studies. But even in its present state, quantum physics points out that both observation and thought play an important role in transforming energy into matter. We do know that the very act of observing an electron causes it to change. Likewise, you don't observe something without first thinking about observing it; observing it also requires thought. Being synergistic it's difficult to distinguish between observation and thought, for they are also two sides of the same coin.

By observing without judgment, we can see clearly and think objectively, and this gives us the ability to choose our desires wisely. *Desire is the magic wave through which thought creates miracles. It is the emotional energy that activates choice.*

I recall a powerful song I sang in church as a child titled "Prayer is the Soul's Sincere Desire." For me, the words were revelatory, describing how prayer (a specific thought) manifests our desires—true prayer is desire. Ponder these words:

Prayer is the soul's sincere desire, uttered or unexpressed.

Emotion of a hidden fire, that trembles in our breast.

There's another new thought to challenge your thinking. Prayer isn't simply bowing your head and saying words. It isn't kneeling beside your bed or standing behind a pulpit, saying words you think you ought to say. Those prayers, lacking real desire and honest emotion, are not prayers at all.

However, there's a catch here. Surely you've noticed that there are times when it seems no matter how much we pray for something we passionately desire, that something never shows up in this world of form. What's happening?

The answer has to do with our two thought systems being in conflict as explained in the dog sled analogy.

When Our Choices Don't Seem to Create What We Want

Imagine a dog sled team of ten dogs, harnessed in two lines of five. When they work together, going in the same direction they are powerful. But what if one set of dogs goes left and the other set of dogs goes right, instead of both going straight ahead.

What happens? *Nothing!* They are at a standstill. Although both sets of dogs are lunging with all their might, the effort of one set of dogs is canceling out the effort of the other set because they are pulling in exact opposite directions; they are going nowhere. Eventually they are exhausted and give up, having accomplished nothing.

It's the same with our thought systems. If we have one thought system desiring and thinking about something it wants, which is the opposite of what the other thought system wants...we have a dog sled condition. Neither thought is going to produce anything for they are working against each other, canceling each other out.

For example, say your conscious mind desires to make a lot of money because all your friends do and you want to keep up with them. Yet your higher mind *doesn't* want the money, knowing the time and energy it will take to create it, knowing how much time it will take away from your spouse and children, knowing how much your spiritual growth would suffer, knowing how much more important all these things are than the money.

Here you have two thought systems, one wanting money and the other rejecting the price of getting it as too high. Your two minds are pulling in opposite directions, each canceling out the energy of the other, just as the two teams of dogs did. To effectively create, we need to get our two thought systems working as a team.

*Until we do this, all the "think and grow rich" books in the total of man's libraries cannot help us create what we want by just **thinking** about our desires.*

To get our two thought systems working as a team, we need to bring our ego, 1% thought system to the truth contained in our higher 99% thought system. We'll learn more about this in "The Technology of Forgiveness" chapter and the "What Is Ego?" chapter.

When man's two thought systems are in sync, it is man's interaction with that quantum wave of possibility that determines what anything becomes, how it manifests. It's the same phenomenon as when man's interaction with the electrons in the experiment changed the outcome of the experiment.

Quantum waves are a way of thinking, possibilities, even probabilities.
—Alan Wolf, quantum physicist

No belief is neutral. Every belief has the power to dictate
each decision you make. For a decision is a conclusion based
on everything that you believe. It is the outcome of belief
and follows it as surely as does suffering follow guilt...
—From *A Course in Miracles*

Chapter Twenty-Two

HOW THOUGHTS
CREATE OUR EXPERIENCE

Unfortunately, as a society, we do not teach our children that they need to tend carefully the garden of their minds. Without structure, censorship, and discipline, our thoughts run on automatic (reactive). Because we have not learned...to manage what goes on inside our brains, we remain vulnerable...
—**Dr. Jill Bolte Taylor**, brain scientist

The Summer Smith Story

Wayne Dyer also reminds us that if you "change your thoughts, you change your life." While he is encouraging you to change your thoughts to improve your life, changing thoughts also has the power to ruin your life—as Summer Smith found out.

Summer Smith is not her real name; it's the name she assumed when she infiltrated the drug culture as an undercover police officer. I heard her tell her story on National Public Radio. She explained that her life was stable before she became Summer Smith. She had a good career with the police force and a significant other whom she loved and planned on reuniting with when her two-year assignment was complete.

Summer knew that in order to be successful in her new role, she would have to think like, feel like, and act like a druggie. That meant wearing dirty, smelly clothes, having wild-unkempt hair, experiencing the feelings of a druggie and acting on those feelings. Summer was a good actor and, as good actors do, she adopted the druggies' way of thinking as well as their way of living. She did it so successfully that she broke up major drug cartels and was instrumental in getting drug kingpins sentenced to prison.

But the results were devastating for Summer personally. Eight months into her intended twenty-four month stint, she couldn't stand it any longer. She felt her true self slipping away and Summer taking over. She had to ask for an early release, and she is still struggling to reconnect to her former self. In the interview, she said it seemed like thinking like a druggie had created permanent changes in her, and she wondered if she can ever return to her former self. She lost her significant other because her thinking and behavior had changed so much she was no longer the person he had fallen in love with. When asked how she felt she had changed she explained, "I am harder than I was."

While I did not know her before, I heard hardness in her voice; I felt her sense of struggle and uneasiness with life and her lack of peace, all of which occurred because she altered her thoughts so completely that they altered her and her life. That's the negative side of what our thoughts can do.

I have no desire to judge Summer's thoughts as wrong because there is a time and a place for everything, and her job called for the change. Some of our most difficult experiences can eventually bring blessings and valuable lessons. I do, however, wish to show by her experience how powerful our thoughts are.

Summer's experience also shows us that it takes time for the permanent change to occur. Although change was gradually occurring from the very first day, it took eight months for her to feel her old self-slipping away.

So remember, if you don't notice immediate obvious change with your efforts to move to 99%, love-based thinking, subtle changes are happening that will show up later. It's important to continue the process for…

Without conscious, ongoing effort to move to 99% thinking, our default mode of thinking takes over. We then unconsciously create another 1% life of fear rather than the life of love we desire.

Brain scientist Dr. Jill Bolte Taylor explains that it is our body's job to keep us safe. Thus, any information received through any of the five senses first goes to the amygdala to be evaluated. The amygdala scans the sensory impression to see if it is like anything it has seen before, then compares it to these past experiences to determine whether it is safe or dangerous. If it thinks it as dangerous, it bypasses the cerebral cortex where it should go for higher processing and instead marches straight to the basal ganglia that houses our survival instincts causing us to react like a frightened animal instead of a logical ethical human being.

Because the amygdala bases all its decisions on past experience it will also interpret something as safe when it is not causing us to walk right into a dangerous trap as my former hairdresser, Debbie, found out.

Debbie's Story

Debbie had an important test at Capitol High School in Boise, Idaho, and found the battery in her car was dead that morning. Unable to find a ride, she decided to hitchhike. A hippy in a dirty, old truck stopped and offered her a ride. This sensory experience passed through her amygdala, which has been preconditioned with negative information about hippies, and flagged it as not a safe ride. She refused the ride.

Next, a nice-looking gentlemen dressed in a suit, driving a clean late-model car offered her a ride. Again, this sensory perception passed through her amygdala, which said, " Clean is good, man in suit is good…plus he looks like your father; this is very good. Her amygdala then sends a message with a "this is a safe ride tag" to the cerebral cortex. Debbie accepts the ride.

To her surprise the gentleman seemed strange. He wouldn't talk, and when they got to the high school and Debbie said, "I get out here," he locked the car door, stepped on the gas, and sped past the school.

Debbie, knowing she was in trouble, reached to unlock the door and jump out, only to find the lock on her side had been removed.

She immediately grabbed the steering wheel, yanked on it over and over, and stamped on her captor's gas-pedal foot in short, quick continual motions causing the car to jerk and zigzag, attempting to draw attention. Finally he slowed down, unlocked the car door, and shoved her out.

When Debbie reported the incident, the policeman said her description fit that of the man they were looking for who had abducted two other girls, who were now presumed dead.

When we are thinking with our biology, it is not only inaccurate; it can be downright dangerous. It nearly cost Debbie her life. See Thought Spiral #1 to see the reactive process in motion.

The Thought Process

Thoughts put energy into motion ("e-motion"). Some of this energy goes out into the quantum soup of universal energy, or the collective unconscious as the famous psychiatrist Carl Jung called it. There it accumulates and affects the whole of humanity as discussed later. Some manifests in our body, creating feelings; our feelings move us to action. Our actions produce certain results or symptoms that become our life. In short...

Thoughts ➔ Feelings ➔ Actions ➔ Results

Reactive thoughts are generally fear based. They cycle through feelings and actions, creating negative results, and then they create more fear—as illustrated in Thought Spiral #1 below.

When you reduce any negative result to its lowest common denominator, you'll find it began with a fear-based thought. Most of our fears evolve around not having enough or not being enough. Reversing reactive thinking is a three-step process.

1. *Do acknowledge* reactive thinking, *recognizing its negative results.*

2. *Undo* the reactive thinking.

3. *Redo* your thinking; create new, healthy proactive thoughts.

Step 1: Do Acknowledge Reactive Thinking

#1 Reactive Thinking

What we *DO*

Thought is king; everything starts with a thought.

Thought Spiral #1 is our Reactive Thought Spiral. It is our automatic unmonitored, uncensored thoughts; our default thinking, which generally dwells on negative victim thoughts and produces unwanted results.

It is our 1% biological-preprogrammed thinking that passes through the fearful amygdala and misinterprets sensory input, which, as Debbie found out, can be not only deceiving but also dangerous.

Reactive Thoughts ➔ Reactive Feelings ➔ Reactive Actions = Negative Results

Step 2: Undo Reactive Thinking

#2   Undoing Reactive Thinking

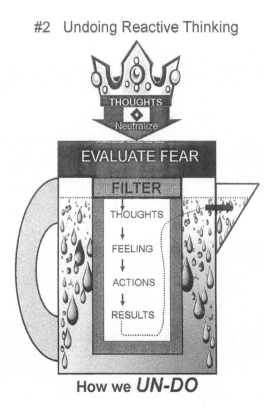

How we *UN-DO*

The Thought Filter illustrates the process of *undoing* the negative effects of our reactive thinking.

Pass your reactive thinking through your Thought Filter. Objectively *evaluate* any negative thoughts you had around the situation you are processing. Then evaluate any feelings those thoughts produced. Next evaluate any negative actions that came from those feelings. Lastly, look carefully at all results and the effect they had on all concerned. By so doing, you become aware of what has not served you. Thank them all for what they have taught you, let them know they are no longer needed, then release them, and let them go. By doing this, you have filtered out the effects of your reactive thoughts and are prepared for Step Three of the process.

Step 3: Creating New Healthy Thinking

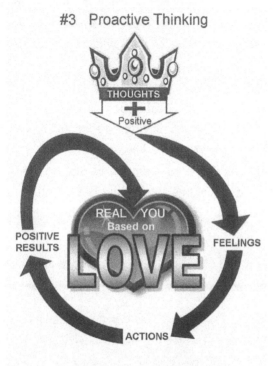

Now you have filtered out the problem thoughts that began the negative cycle, you can change them, gaining control of your life.

Now, choose a new healthy thought, go clockwise around the Thought Spiral #2, as seen above. You *choose* a new thought. Don't allow your biology to choose for you. Notice the feelings your new thought creates and the actions and results that follow.

Proactive Thoughts ➔ Proactive Feelings ➔ Proactive Actions = Positive Results

Hint: If you have a tendency towards anger or other negative emotions, don't react to them for 90 seconds. The biological feeling will then dissipate, giving you a choice about whether you will react or be proactive.

Now put yourself in George's world (see below), taking the role of his mother, creating a virtual experience of using the three-step process to turn a negative situation into a positive one. *This virtual exercise is designed to help you experience the transformation that can take place by using this process.*

George's World and How It Transformed

Here's the case of the hypothetical George and you as his hypothetical mom. George is outside in the warm sun playing baseball and hits a home run. But the ball goes through a neighbor's plate-glass window. You watch it happen. It's a huge window and you know it is going to be very expensive to replace, and your family is already struggling financially. While you're thinking about the window, George runs home and runs up to his bedroom and slams the door. You do nothing.

Using Thought Spiral #1. As George's mother, follow it counter-clockwise to experience how this incident of reactive behavior created negative results.

You remember your first *thought* was "Oh no, my son has broken a neighbor's very expensive window." The *feeling* that followed was fear of the financial responsibility, so the *action* you take is really a *reaction, one generated from a fear thought*. The *results* show up later. Your reaction was to ignore the whole thing and pretend you don't know anything about it. You thought, "No one was home and they'll never know who broke the window." What will be the *result* of your *action* or more accurately, your *reaction*?

Remember that any action or reaction generated from fear will eventually end up with a negative result, although that result may not show up immediately.

Two weeks later, George gets caught shoplifting and is taken to juvenile court. You feel terrible, recognizing there could be a connection between the broken window and his acting-out now. After castigating yourself for not addressing the window incident properly, you wonder what you can you do to change the results that came from this reactive action over the broken window.

You look at the Thought Filter model, which visually shows you that, by recognizing and evaluating your fears, you can filter out those impure fear thoughts that created the impure feelings and actions. In this way, you can neutralize the effects of the reactive thinking.

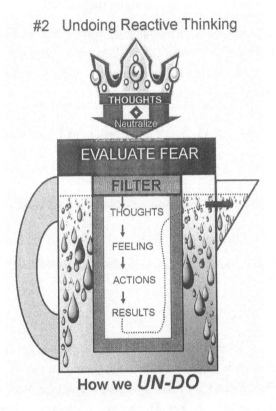

#2   Undoing Reactive Thinking

How we *UN-DO*

Together you and George use the Thought Filter to evaluate your reactive behavior in the following manner:

- <u>Observing and thinking about his *results*:</u> George realizes he wants his life to change directions. You tell George that you feel partly responsible. You confess you watched the ball go through the window and admit your actions were irresponsible. You explain that you know you should have confronted him and expected him to be responsible for his actions. Wringing your hands, you further explain you're concerned that letting him get away with breaking the window could have been an underlying factor that led to his shoplifting.

- Observing and thinking about his *actions:* George hangs his head and confesses that his actions were also irresponsible, that he should have been responsible and told you about the window.

- Observing and thinking about your *feelings*: You engage George in a dialogue that brings you closer. You both recognize that George felt scared, afraid to face the consequences, and reacted to his fears rather than thinking proactively.

You ask, "What were we thinking that would make us react as we did?"

George responds: "I was thinking that Dad would ground me for a very long time and I had some special sports events coming up that I just couldn't miss, plus I knew he'd make me pay for the window and I just didn't have the money."

You respond, "So your bottom-line thinking was that getting immediate gratification for your wants was more important than being honest and responsible?"

George again hangs his head.

You continue, "But you're just a kid trying to grow up. Kids make mistakes and so do adults. I knew you didn't have the money to pay for the window and we would probably have to pay for it. I was also afraid we didn't have the money. But my thinking error goes deeper. The bottom line was my fear of 'not enough' caused me to react in a manner that was damaging to you. I'm so sorry!"

"I'm sorry, too, Mother," George says. Feeling closer than you ever have, you embrace each other, both feeling better for facing yourselves and your problems honestly. Then he confesses that she was right about the connection between the window and the shoplifting. *"I thought because I got away with breaking the window, I could get away with the shoplifting."*

You say, "We are so fortunate that Judge Anderson dismissed the shoplifting charge in lieu of community service. I think he could sense that you were truly repentant—which I also believe; I'm very proud of you."

Proactive Behavior and the Thought Spiral

After undoing the effects of your reactions, neutralizing them using the Thought Filter, you turn to Thought Spiral #2. You begin by choosing a new positive, proactive thought. This will automatically create positive feelings and actions, which will then create the positive results you desire. *As always, you begin at the thought spot.*

#3   Proactive Thinking

What we *RE-DO*

"I *think* we can create the money to pay for the window. Let's think it through. How can you earn the money to pay for the window when you're not old enough to get a job?" (*Creating a new thought*)

Both you and George are now *feeling* hopeful about the future and feeling much better about yourselves after deciding to take responsibility. (*New thoughts create new feelings*)

After batting ideas around for a few minutes, George comes up with a good one. "I have a friend whose dad owns a car wash. I think he might give me a job just long enough to pay for the Isaaksons' window," he said.

"That's a great suggestion, George, I'm so pleased with the way you are handling the problem and the responsibility you're taking. Go see Mr. Abbott after school tomorrow, ask him about work, and tell him why you need the money."

George did just that and was ecstatic at Mr. Abbot's response, as he reports to you that evening. *(Creating new actions)*

"Mr. Abbott not only gave me a job, Mom, he told me how commendable he thought it was that I was taking responsibility for the window; he said I'm the kind of man he would like to have date his daughter. He called me a man, Mom, and I'm only eleven. I've always had a crush on his daughter! When I get into high school, I'm going to ask her to the prom." George didn't stop smiling the remainder of the day, nor did you. *(Creating New Results)*

Using the thought wheel proactively is simple but not always easy. Yet it's important to understand how everything begins with a thought. When you change your thoughts, you change your life. Summer Smith taught us how thoughts can destroy a life. George and his mother taught us how thoughts can improve a life.

I'll remind you again that beliefs are simply thoughts we think over and over until they become beliefs.

XYB Exercise

When you are feeling victimized, depressed or out of sorts, it's simply because...you are indulging in 1% thoughts that you believe have validity. These feelings may be emerging from past repressed feelings or present circumstances. *They are showing up to give you an opportunity to examine your dysfunctional beliefs.* Caution: Do not send them back underground by judging or ignoring them. If you don't deal with them, they will deal with you and create more negatives in your life until they get your attention once and for all. They are coming up for healing to allow you to discover the real healthy, happy you. Listen carefully to them. Then do your XYB exercise.

Xamine **Y**our **B**eliefs. Objectively notice the 1% thoughts that are behind your negative feelings. Discern the thoughts that formed the beliefs. *Your feelings are your barometer, showing you where your thoughts are on the Love-Fear scale.* The better you feel, the closer you are to love. The worse you feel, the closer you are to fear. After detecting your culprit 1% fear thoughts, replace them with 99% love thoughts; new feelings, actions and results will follow. Fear thoughts (beliefs) don't feel good. They may cause you to lose your hair.

This is your 1% mind.

Chapter Twenty-Three:
WHEN ENOUGH IS NEVER ENOUGH

*...Not all people's idols are the same, but they all have one
thing in common...more...[there] must be more. It does not
really matter more of what; more beauty, more
intelligence, more wealth...But more of something...*
—From *A Course in Miracles*

Chapter Twenty-One showed us how our thoughts create our life. Chapter Twenty-Two validated that idea with scientific research. This chapter reveals where most of our thoughts are now. Understanding our addiction to more, then overcoming that addiction, can be as freeing as being rescued from quicksand.

My cherished experience with the indigenous group of Huichol Indians in the Sierra Madres mountains in Mexico confronted me with how subtly my thoughts had been sucked into this "not enough, there must be more" culture, as most of us have been. That realization was a blessing that would prepare me for a huge lifestyle change I was about to experience. My work with this Indian tribe became a life-changing experience—one that taught me to look at money, and life, differently. It highlighted my previously darkened vision that prevented me from seeing that our society idolizes *more*; we've created and worship the

God "Wantmore," which made me ask myself, "What message are we giving ourselves when we think we must always have more, *more* of something?"

The answer came quickly:

It means we don't feel we are good enough if we don't have enough, because we have come to equate our self-worth with our net worth.

This mentality keeps us imprisoned in the 1% ego world of fear.

Psychologist Dr. Lee Jampolsky puts it this way: "Most of the time from the ego's default operating system, which can be thought of as 'wrong-mindedness,' the unconscious questions you ask as you start your day are, 'What am I *not* getting?' Or 'What am I lacking that I need and seem to want?' *If you look closely, you will see the origin of all negative thinking begins there.*"

"The ego often plants the assumption that 'I never get what I really want [or enough of what I really want].'" So it seems that our minds and lives evolve around not having enough. How many times have you awakened in the morning, maybe a little late, and began your day with some of the following thought patterns?

"The crappy old alarm, something is wrong with it, it went off late, I *need a better one*...now I won't have *enough time* for breakfast. Oh well, I probably *don't have enough* milk for my cereal anyway and when I get to work I've got so much work I probably *won't have enough time* to take a break and get something to eat, then the thought occurs to you when you get in the car to go to work that you probably *don't have enough gas* to get to work. You know you should have filled it earlier but were concerned that you *wouldn't have enough money* to get you to your next paycheck if you filled it up, and chide yourself for *not having enough good sense* to at least put a few gallons of gas in it. As you pull out of your driveway, you look down at the outfit you put on and say, "I hate this old dress; I just *don't have enough decent clothes* to appear professional on my job."

So our main focus in life is on what we lack. But, we reason, one thing could fix everything, if we had had enough of it. That one thing would be m-o-n-e-y, for it is the universally accepted commodity, which can be traded for anything else we want or need—that's why we created it.

Our focus now begins to revolve around the lack of m-o-n-e-y; we must have more if we are going to have enough to make us be enough, to make us okay. Money, after all, can buy us power, prestige, big houses, fancy cars, even a new face or body if we have enough to pay a plastic surgeon. Money can even buy us friends—maybe not the right kind of friends, but friends nevertheless.

Most of modern society allows our self-worth to be determined by how much money we have. If we always need more, that means we never have enough which means, and I'll repeat it, *we are not enough*! This means we have no genuine self-esteem. It is this poor self-esteem, the fear of not being enough that motivates much of our 1% fear-based thinking.

Then out of fear, we begin to accumulate and hoard our money. Yet, as Gertrude, whom we met in Chapter Thirteen, so wisely told us, money is like water and needs to flow where it is needed. If it doesn't keep moving it becomes stagnant and toxic. Hoarding money is like stopping the flow of water, making it toxic to those who "own" it.

We know blood also becomes toxic if it isn't allowed to continually flow through the body's filters, the lymph nodes, the liver, etc. If the channels through which blood flows—the arteries and veins—get clogged up with plaque, preventing it from flowing, in addition to becoming toxic, it can cause heart attacks or strokes and even kill. Hoarding money or accumulating excess can have a toxic effect on our body and a deadly effect on our spirit.

There's still another problem. If we don't allow money to flow to the place it can do the most good—spiritual organizations, charities, homeless, and other projects that advance the well being of our fellow humans, etc.—we can become obsessed with using our money to accumulate stuff for ourselves. We become so attached to our possessions and not ever having enough that it takes all our time and energy to:

1. Earn the money to buy more,

2. Shop till you drop to find all the things we want to spend it for,

3. Then to take care of all the things you've bought.

All that getting and spending never satisfies, for you cannot fill a hole on the inside with anything from the outside.

When these things fail to make us feel okay, we look for more of something else. This search, this addiction for more, robs us of our very lives that could be used to enjoy our family and friends, experience the beauty of nature, learn something new, do something productive to help others, our country, etc. Here we find true wealth not on our balance sheet.

Life has thrown experiences my way that allowed me to confront my own lack of balance living in a culture of "not enough"; the Huichol experience was one of them. Section One revealed the same truth through a more negative experience, which I needed to remind me that I had slipped back into my default 1% thinking.

After identifying the problem of our "not enough" addiction, Dr. Jampolsky suggests some solutions for undoing this pattern with "right-minded" thinking.

Step One of "right-mindedness," or loving fully, is to *choose* to love where you are, who you are and what you are. It is the opposite of the ego's default focus on what you are *not* getting or not getting enough of.

Step Two: Expand that beautiful moment into loving the work you will do today, no matter what it is. Love where you live, love your neighbors without insisting they change.

Step Three: Love what doesn't seem so wonderful, knowing what seems to be trauma is truly a blessing, knowing that all things work to the good of those who love. Find the ability to love within the challenge, even love those who are challenging. In the morning upon awaking, say the following words, even if you don't mean them—yet.

"I am letting go today, forgiving, for I realize the pain held shall become the suffering that keeps me from my greatest good."

Step Four: Be loving to all in your life without any expectation of how they will respond. Allow people, and yourself, to be who they are, and how they are. Allow them to learn their own lessons without judgment and stand witness to the light within them.

When we master all this we will have moved from 1% to 99% thinking, from the illusion of fear to the reality of love. We will no longer be caught in the "I'm not enough because I don't have enough syndrome," even if all our toys disappear along with the money we used to purchase them. Surviving it all begins with a change of thinking. A friend who had lost $20 million looked at it philosophically and said, *"Freedom's just another word for nothing left to lose."*

My experience with the Huichol was an example of learning from those who may not be rich in money, but are nevertheless wealthy in ways in which we're impoverished and have much to teach us. Here's how psychologist and one-time atheist Helen Schucman put it.

> *In my hands is everything you want and need and hoped*
> *To find among the shabby toys of earth.*
> *I take them all from you and they are gone.*
> *And shining in the place where once they stood there*
> *Is a gateway to another world*
> *Through which we enter in the name of God.*

Helen's message is clear. We can't find our 99% world until we step out of our 1% world of addiction to things. We may kick and scream when circumstances take those things from us, but when we've finished our tantrums, we can look past what we thought was trauma and see the blessing. Shining in the place where our stuff once stood, we find a gateway to another world, our 99% world, our original home.

> *If a person gets his attitude toward money straight,*
> *it will help straighten out almost every other area in his life.*
> **—Rev. Billy Graham**

> *I know of no more encouraging fact than the unquestionable*
> *ability of man to elevate his life by conscious endeavor.*
> **—Henry David Thoreau**

Chapter Twenty-Four

WHAT IS EGO?

...The ego tells you that by following its fear-based ways,
it will get you what you think you want, yet still
perpetuates the belief that you will never get what you want.
—Psychologist **Lee Jampolsky**

We hang onto [negative] ego for two reasons:
Either we cannot see it, or we're afraid to let go of it.
—**Rabbi Yehuda Berg**

Let's begin our exploration of ego with these thoughts from Jampolsky, a spiritual psychologist, and Berg, a Jewish mystic. We've alluded to ego and even described it as our fear thought system. Let's explore it further.

Understanding the ego is the first step in conquering it. Conquering it opens the door to permanent peace and prosperity.

From Dr. Jampolsky's insights, we see that the ego is definitely not our friend, not something we want to keep. From Kabbalist Yehuda Berg's insights, we can see why we won't let go of it. We know it's destructive, but why do we have it, and how do we identify it, or overcome our fear of it so we can get rid of it? Do we love it, hate it, try to kill it, make friends with it, ignore it, forgive it, or what? This had been a heavy topic of conversation among my A *Course in Miracles* (ACIM) group.

Most of our ACIM group understood ego as our fear thought system, in constant survival mode, always out for itself alone. But that didn't explain exactly why we have an ego, where it came from and how it got to be so negative and fearful. I had too little information about ego to satisfy my soul.

I didn't get the missing pieces until Jody, a member of our ACIM spiritual movie group, dropped some information right in my lap, just when I needed it. After we'd eaten and just before we started our movie, Jody leaned over the red oak railing that divided the dining area from the family room, rested her hand on the rust leather sofa on which I sat and said, "I have a movie on *Releasing Negative Ego*. I think you'll want to see it and decide if you want to use it for our movie night next month."

The concept of *Negative* Ego intrigued me; it implied there must be somewhere its opposite, a positive ego, a new thought to me. Jodi went to the car and came back with the VHS video. It was an old, old recording, so old I couldn't find anything on the Internet about it, nothing in used and rare books, and nothing on rare videos. Yet in this old video, I found our Lazarus interpretation of *why we have our ego, where it came from and why it got to be so fearful.* I also found in his explanation of ego, the key to undoing it.

In addition to the mystical information I'd studied and what Jodi provided, more information jumped out of a Kabbalistic CD I had in my car and from a newsletter I just happened to read, which I generally throw away. Now I'll synthesize the information, couple it with my own experience, and take on the monumental task of explaining ego from an entirely new perspective.

Why Do We Have an Ego?

To explain, we must go back to why we came to this planet. We came here to develop our divine potential and find our way back home. However, when we got here we found it quite overwhelming. There was so much to take in, so much that we needed to understand. So, according to Lazarus, we created an assistant to gather information and bring it to us for interpretation. We developed our ego as our information gatherer and mailman.

That originally was its only function. Ego's function was never to examine the content, interpret the information it gathered, or decide what to do with it. That was the function of our 99% mind. So originally we created our ego as a positive assistant, then it became a dreaded opponent. How did it happen?

The ego, like a spoiled child, wanted more and more control and we as an indulgent, and perhaps a lazy or more likely, a fearful parent, allowed it to take on more and more responsibility that was to have been carried out by our 99% mind.

Did we lose track of our negative ego, or did we become afraid of it, or both? Or did we get overwhelmed at the awesome job of interpreting everything our ego brought us? Perhaps we haven't looked for answers very hard because we're glad to let the ego do all the work of not only gathering and delivering information, but also interpreting its content and form. Or did we just get tired of fighting this persistent spoiled child who wanted more and more control, and simply give in? Most likely, the best answer is "all of the above."

Whatever the case, it was this relinquishment of responsibility that turned our little helper, the ego, into something negative, fearful, and vicious. It wasn't equipped to handle all this responsibility. It was like allowing, or encouraging, a five year old to teach school with adults as the students. It couldn't do the job. We had put the mailman in charge of our lives, continually promoting it until it rose to what the Peter Principle would call the level of its incompetence. This made it afraid of the responsibility, feeling unequipped to handle it. But ego was too proud to let it go because it loved the control. In its new position of being in control, yet being terrified, it became our antagonist.

Once the mistake was made, it was difficult to fix, much like trying to get an out-of-control, spoiled child to stop throwing temper tantrums. And each time we gave in to our ego child, it gained more and more strength and we got weaker and became more and more afraid.

QUESTION: So what happened to us, these divine, powerful beings with all the DNA potential of our creator? What caused us to weaken and become so afraid that we allowed this Negative ego to evolve and get so out of control?

ANSWER: When we came to this planet, we gradually forgot who we were. As babies we felt connected to everything, yet we were helpless and had to rely on others to teach us how to survive. But survival skills did not teach us anything about how to handle the ego. They taught us what we had to do to stay in harmony, or at least out of trouble, with those adults around us. The adults around us informed us how we could do just that.

Our parents would say, "Do as you're told!"

Our teachers would say, "Don't ask questions, just do your assignment."

Society would say, "Just be like everyone else, fit in, be normal."

Our boss would say, "Do the job as I tell you to."

So we developed a fear of thinking for ourselves and doing anything contrary to the wishes of those adult controllers in our lives. It wasn't safe. If we did, our parents could punish us, our teachers could give us bad grades, society could refuse to accept us, or our boss could fire us. So our life experiences have put us in fear of thinking for ourselves, which puts us on the same fear wavelength as ego. Our fear has made us one with the ego since like energies connect. Being one with our ego, we have been wallowing around in our egoness ever since, allowing it do our thinking for us. This caused us to forget who we really are, a DNA offspring of our creator, with divine potential.

Let me emphasize this: *The ego doesn't know how to really think.* Although it tries, it is always confused and messes everything up. Thus we have the kind of world we have with little real *proactive thinking* going on, the kind of thinking that will solve problems. *Ego always reacts* for it has no real thinking skills to proactively solve problems. It remains in fear, producing what fear inevitably produces: chaos, uncertainty and eventually disintegration.

In addition to, or maybe because of these fears, we added one more: the fear of letting go of the past and growing up. To grow up would require that we take responsibility and develop some mature adult thinking; yet we've been trained to be afraid to really think for ourselves. And if we grew up, we'd have to deal with our own problems and pain, and our own joy. We couldn't hide behind victim and stay a helpless child while masquerading as an adult in a grown-up body.

How Ego Works to Deceive

While our negative ego-self is not good at real thinking, it is good at survival. It wants the job security of controlling our lives. If it revealed its true nature we'd dismiss it immediately, so it presents itself as a faithful friend. It is the known; it is what is comfortable. It protects us from painful situations with what psychologists call defense mechanisms, which include both healthy and harmful ways to cope with stress.

Harmful defense mechanisms include:

- Rationalization (rational lies)
- Repression (unconscious stuffing of painful impulses, desires, or fears)
- Suppression (the conscious stuffing of unacceptable thoughts or desires)
- Denial ("I don't have a problem")
- Projection ("You have the problem")

These defense mechanisms are all ways of avoiding painful situations. But life teaches us if you don't deal with a situation up front and try to hide from it, it will come back as a monster to consume you.

This is one way the ego lies to make you think it is your friend. It entices you to go for the instant gratification, to blame someone else, to take the easy way out. In the long run, that's the hard way out, if you get out at all. Denial and avoidance cause the problem to return, bigger and often unrecognizable, making the origin of the problem difficult to find, unravel and solve.

Burying problems in our unconscious is much like sprinkling weed seeds among flower seeds in fertile soil. They all grow, intermingle, change forms, produce more seeds that fall into the fertile soil of the mind, making it very difficult to tell the weeds from the flowers. The best solution, don't plant the seeds—*don't listen to ego when it tells you to take the easy way out.* Solve the problem up front and don't deny it or hide it. Otherwise it's like trying to get rid of a weed in a garden by burying its seeds.

It's useful to use the analogy of the frog in the pot. If you put a frog in a pot of warm water and turn up the heat a degree a day for a few weeks, the frog hardly notices…until one day the water is near boiling and kills the frog. This is how ego uses our defense mechanisms to survive. It tries to kill our spirit for it knows once we find our true spirit, we'll drop negative ego as fast as we would a poisonous snake. It knows if it were to throw us into boiling water all at once, we'd jump out, so it lulls us into carnal security. It soothes us, saying all is well, while it rushes us down to incompetence, pain and even death. Ego will do what it has to do to survive and maintain control of our lives; it never tells us the truth; it's always confused.

We wanted life to be simple truths and sweet platitudes. We wanted it to be easy. That is what ego promised. By accepting ego's lies and half-truths, we became more and more emotionally crippled as we became more separated from our real selves and become increasingly one with our ego. And being in ego, we became increasingly fearful. Being in fear, we couldn't forgive and return to love.

While each ego is unique and develops its own personality, there are some general categories in which it functions.

How Negative Ego Manifests

1. *Encourages false superiority, based on a hidden fear of not being good enough:* "I don't need your help, I can do it alone, I'm bigger, better and smarter than any of you." This separates you from your brother.

2. *Encourages inferiority:* "I'm inferior, I'm a helpless victim, I'm not good enough, and I'm not deserving." This can manifest in a variety of ways: depression, dependency, not succeeding. Ego wants us to die a pauper, but it will tell us it wants the opposite.

3. *Fosters mistrust of self and self-worth:* Ego tells us that if we are anything short of perfection we not good enough and aren't worthy to give or receive love.

4. *Refuses satisfaction:* "I never get what I really want."

5. *Doesn't think things through*: The ego has no real thinking skills. Being reactive, it is always the victim, the acted upon, it is never the actor, the creator of anything; it just reacts to what already has been created.

6. *Promises the moon but delivers nothing:* Ego lies to you because it can't think straight. When you do something wrong, it tells you it is right.

When you do something right, it tells you it is wrong. Anything the ego creates is not sustainable, whether it's money, a relationship, anything.

Overcoming Negative Ego

Now that we know how ego developed, we have a clue about how to overcome it. Once we understand that ego is in fear for its own survival, we simply need to take it out of survival mode, which will take it out of fear. *Without fear, the ego would not be the negative ego anymore.* Fear is to the ego what breath is to the body; it keeps our ego thought system alive.

How do we take ego out of fear? Here are six suggestions:

- *Own it.* Don't be in denial that you are being controlled by ego; we all are, to one degree or another. Any negative feeling or negative act is born of ego.

- *Identify your ego's personality.* Create a body for your ego, give it all your negative traits, write it into a play or a scene and see how it acts. This will help you identify how your ego is working to sabotage your life. Does it act "better than," or does it feign false humility and act "less than" because it feels" better than." Does it play victim, thinking everyone else is doing "it" to them? Is it afraid of love, or is it addicted to what it thinks is love, etc?

- *Identify the short- and long-term results of negative ego's control of our life.* What effect does it have on your relationships? What effect does it have on your finances, your health and your future?

- *Continually forgive yourself and others.* More on the importance of that in the following forgiveness chapter.

- *Handle positive results through your 99% mind.* This keeps you from falling back into negative ego, feeling "better than."

- *Make a choice.* Am I going to be *done* with negative ego, or am I going to be *done in* by it? See more in the "Creating Miracles" chapter.

Building Positive Ego

Once you eliminate negative ego, you leave a vacuum that must be filled. You must fill it with something positive, or negative ego will step back in that space and take control again. The following are helps for filling in the empty space:

- *Recommit to being done with negative ego.* Commitment is a promise you make to yourself; it is a powerful thing. When we don't keep our commitment to self, we begin distrusting ourselves as we would any other person who makes a commitment to us and defaults.

- *Keep an eye on the negative ego.* You have already put it outside and separate from yourself by personifying it. Make certain it doesn't again try to take over.

- *Get help from your divine self to keep ego in control.* Your negative ego self is surely not going to help you; it will fight you.

- *Determine what life looks like with a positive ego.* Write down all the things you want in your positive ego. Remember that positive ego's only function is to be an information gatherer. Don't allow it to interpret the information it brings to you, or tell you how it should be used. Remember, that is the business of your 99% mind.

- *Your positive ego's role is to interact with the world, gathering information. Recreate ego into a joyful mailman.* Personify your positive ego as a person outside you, just as you did your negative ego. Teach it to feel joy, to experience laughter, to love dance and nature; teach it growth can be joyous.

Creating a Space for Love

- When you first wake up, empty any fears you may have by saying this fear is not real because I'm concerned about something that hasn't happened yet, so it's a creation of the ego, all smoke and mirrors, simply an illusion.

- Having eliminated fear, you have created a space for love to enter. Immediately focus on loving where you are and who you are. See all your positive characteristics. Look at all your talents and accomplishments, no matter how small they seem.

- When you become skilled at that, expand your love and appreciation. Love what you do and where you do it. Love the people you do it with without them having to change first.

- Then expand your love to all that doesn't seem wonderful. Know that behind every challenge is a blessing. Know that the challenge is a gift that can teach great lessons and bring peace. Know that by going through the wormhole in every black hole, you'll find a whole new universe.

- Do your best every day and be grateful for each accomplishment without being attached to the form it takes or the outcome.

- Be compassionate and helpful with others who are having challenges and need help, but do not take them on as your problems. These problems were, in some mysterious way, created especially for their learning; for you to take them on is to take away the lessons and blessings they were intended to create for that person.

The Love Icon Program

When you get good at the above transformational steps, here's a way to simplify them.

- Create two icons: a frowny face for your negative ego and a smiley face for the real you. Call the first icon fear and call the second love. Into the love icon program all the above steps. Imagine the icons side by side as if on a computer screen. Keep an eye on them. Our fear icon has the ability to self-activate. If that happens, see yourself with a computer mouse clicking and deleting the fear icon and then clicking and activating the love icon. By now you have the above steps memorized and clicking your love icon will activate them.

- If you still are not feeling good, do the XYB process in Chapter Twenty-Two.

Until we get negative ego under control, we can trick it and use it in a positive way to help us grow past it. Anytime we have negative feelings, we know we are in ego. We can ask our higher self to help us understand what fear or judgment is coming up, to show us what needs to be healed—then get quiet and listen for the answer. Then forgive the thought that created the feeling. (See more on the power of real forgiveness in Chapter Twenty-Five) In this way, we remove one more veil that separates us from our real, powerful self.

Recognizing and overcoming negative ego is absolutely essential if you truly desire personal growth and peace. You either bust negative ego, or build it. Nothing ever stands still; it goes either forward or backward. Remember, perfect love casts out fear. When working with ego, as when working with an out of control child, you must act in the spirit of tough love. Don't allow ego to control your life. Remove some of the pressure you've put on it by taking back your own responsibilities, and like an unruly child, it will become more compliant.

This whole book has been written to polish the mirror and present you with choices, ways of thinking and being that will allow you to move out of this ego world of chaos and fear to a higher place of peace and prosperity, a place of genuine love.

These are the blessings and lessons that lurked behind the metaphor of the Phoenix being burned in the funeral pyre and rising again. We might call it going through the refiner's fire and coming out a new transformed person.

It's because of the traumas I've experienced that I know what I know about the rebirth of the Phoenix as it rises from ashes and identify with the words of Bill W., co-founder of Alcoholics Anonymous, who said,

"Years ago I used to commiserate with all those people who suffered. Now I commiserate only with those who suffer in ignorance, who do not understand the purpose and ultimate utility of pain."

What do you choose from here? Your choice determines your life.

Chapter Twenty-Five

THE TECHNOLOGY OF FORGIVENESS

Forgiveness is always a gift you give to yourself,
not the person you think you are forgiving.
—**Gary R. Renard**, author of *Your Immortal Reality*

Life is for giving love. For giving. For giving love.
That is forgiveness, nothing else.
—**Roger Lamphear,** author of Unified

There are myriad books written about fear; there are many written about love. To my knowledge, the only books that can tell you how to get from one place to the other…are written by mystics.

So how do you get from the world of fear to the world of love? I knew if I searched long enough I'd find one simple answer. After over twenty years of searching, I believe *forgiveness is the bottom-line answer*, forgiveness of self as well as others. This answer was there all along, but it had been so distorted by ego, I couldn't recognize it. I'm talking about a new of kind forgiveness not distorted by ego thinking. I'm talking about a forgiveness few have experienced, one you'll seek out once you recognize how *it can free you from limitations*. Our old 1% forgiveness model has no power. Come with me and witness 1% ego forgiveness in progress and notice the results.

Patrick and Paul

Patrick is about to "forgive" an employee who made a serious mistake. There he is, in his freshly ironed shirt, matching tie and crisply creased khakis, walking out of his million-dollar, designer-decorated house. He's about to get into his Mercedes to drive to his employee's modest home to forgive him for a mistake he'd made on the books, creating problems with a merger in process. When he arrives at Paul's home, Patrick confidently strides up the sidewalk and rings Paul's doorbell.

Paul, the employee, answers the door in his tattered Levis and flannel shirt, looking very dejected. He invites Patrick to come in. As Patrick enters, he notices Paul's boys wrestling on the floor with the dog while his two-year-old daughter is playing with toys she's scattered on the floor.

Patrick the Offended looks around and says nothing but thinks, "This place is such a mess. I'm certainly glad my place doesn't look like this." Then he gets down to business, feeling quite righteous about what he is about to do. He says, "Paul, you know how upset I've been about your bookkeeping error. I was going to deduct from your pay what it cost me, but I've decided to forgive you instead and keep your present salary intact."

Paul the Offender sits there trying to feel grateful, but somehow he still feels ashamed, guilty and "less than."

Reflect on what has just happened here. Is it anything that looks like real resolution, healing or unity? First, the "old forgiveness" is taking place externally, on the level of form; real forgiveness begins as an internal process, for both the offender and the offended. The problem with this ego forgiveness is that it focuses on the offender and his problem rather than the internal process that can free both the offender and the offended from guilt and shame. While the offended may not have guilt over this matter, every human soul on this planet has unresolved guilt. (That's a story for another day.) For the offended, true forgiveness can mean freedom from other unconscious, repressed guilt.

Shame and Guilt

Psychiatrist Dr. David Hawkins explains further why this 1% forgiveness, such as we have just witnessed, cannot possibly work. He's created a consciousness scale that ranges from 20 to 1,000, with 1,000 being Christ Consciousness and guilt and shame, at 20 and 30, the lowest energies on the scale. What this means is the more conscious you are, the more empowered and emotionally healthy you are, the more connected you are to the real you. It also means that it's impossible for someone living in shame and guilt to access the level of consciousness needed to reconnect to their source, for according to wave physics, only like energies (waves) can connect. If you reduce all matter to its common denominator, it's all wave energy.

Forgiveness will be a major step in reconnecting us to who we really are, to reconnecting us to the love wavelength. The ego mind has distorted the true meaning of forgiveness as it does everything, until what was meant to heal, does the opposite. Let's look a little further into how ego distorts and destroys the forgiveness process.

One form of 1% ego forgiveness essentially says, "Even though you are guilty, I am a much bigger and better person, so I (the superior) am going to forgive you (the inferior)." What does this do? It strengthens ego, creates more guilt and fear in the "forgivee" and a false sense of superiority in the "forgiver." This is the scenario we just described with Patrick and Paul.

Another form lacks the blatant arrogance of the first. The forgiver doesn't blame the forgivee alone; he blames himself too, saying they are both sinners and deserve the wrath of God. This puts them both into fear of not being okay. Fear always separates one from himself, from each other and from God. This form passes itself off as humility and charity instead of what it is: cruelty to both parties.

A similar form of 1% forgiveness creates a martyr who dons the face of suffering and pain as silent proof he has accepted his guilt and will suffer the consequences by forever carrying the big scarlet "A" on his back so he can be forgiven.

Others will consent to trading their freedom for the release of their sins. The offended might say, or imply, "I will forgive you if you meet my needs, for in your slavery is my release." My inner self looks at this and says, "There is no real forgiveness, or release, for either the offended or the offendee in emotional blackmail."

Unity, or becoming one, is what Jesus Christ preached; it's what eastern religions preach; it's what many metaphysical and new age religions preach. So how do we get to 99% forgiveness and unity?

True 99% forgiveness is as different from 1% forgiveness as a butterfly is from a rock. One keeps you stuck in one place, the other allows you to fly high and see far. It lifts you to your place of empowerment. Again, delete any previous ideas about the value of 1% "rock" forgiveness; these ideas just keep you stuck.

A New Kind of Forgiveness

We must learn to practice a forgiveness that removes the judgments and guilt that keep us separated from our brother, our maker and ourselves. We'll see that this new forgiveness is a gift in so many ways.

It removes the blocks to our own personal power, gives us personal peace, and produces peace in the world. Then we understand we are truly dealing with a new kind of forgiveness.

It lifts another veil or curtain that stands between us and the 99% world of truth.

This New Forgiveness heals the hidden guilt that separates us from who we really are.

This New Forgiveness eliminates suffering more rapidly than anything else.

This New Forgiveness gives us freedom from our limited selves.

This New Forgiveness is an actual *technology*, which opens the door to hidden truth.

But heaven knows what price to put on its goods. To activate this new kind of forgiveness, we must be *willing* to open our minds to embrace critical truths that may first shock and then disturb but ultimately set us free.

There are two more critical truths we must comprehend if we are to effectively use this kind of forgiveness to buy us freedom from our limited selves. If I hadn't received it through direct revelation and later validated it through my study and research, I would have had a difficult time believing the first one myself.

Critical Truth #1: Our judgments are really projections of our own guilt onto another person. Ouch!

Critical Truth #2: We must find the thought that caused the wrong action and forgive and change that thought. Trying to forgive the wrong action doesn't work. Wow!

> *You never hate your brother for his sins, but only for your own. Whatever form his sins appear to take, it but obscures the fact that you believe [them] to be yours...*

> *If you didn't believe you deserved attack [anything one says or does to diminish or harm themselves or another], it would never occur to you to give attack to anyone at all.*

> —From *A Course in Miracles*

> *Always remember that forgiveness that leads to this experience [of awakening] must be done at the level of cause [thought] and not effect [form].*
> **—Gary Renard**

Your Immortal Reality

What exactly is Gary Renard saying about forgiveness work being done at the level of cause and not effect? It means essentially the same thing as Critical Truth #1. If you are in need of forgiving yourself, for example, don't forgive the thing you think you did wrong; that's the *effect*. Instead, forgive the thought that began the process that resulted in your wrong action; that's the *cause*. When you isolate the cause-thought, study it, think on it, and recognize its flaws. Then let it go and replace it with a healthy thought. This is so essential to understand, I'll say it another way.

Most people struggling with forgiveness try to forgive the problem. This does not work; we must get to the cause of the problem and forgive that. The cause always starts with a thought. Thus we must isolate the thought that caused us to behave badly.

Understanding the thought wheel in the previous chapter explains why forgiveness can't be effective at the behavior level, for behavior always follows thought. Yet for the New Forgiveness to be effective both Critical Truth # 1 must be understood and Critical Truth #2 must be employed to be successful, as you'll see in the following story.

The Case of the Clothing Judgment

Years ago, I'd tried to forgive a woman in my church I couldn't stand, but I simply couldn't seem to stop judging her as narcissistic, selfish, and snooty long enough to accomplish the task. Paula never put on an extra ounce, always looked picture-perfect with her Fifth Avenue wardrobe, Italian shoes and immaculately groomed hair. Her wardrobe budget would have nicely supported a small family. Worst of all, she acted as if she were a cut above the rest.

I continually judged Paula's behavior as narcissistic and overindulgent, and then I judged myself for being so judgmental. I didn't like her, and I didn't like myself for not liking her. I kept trying to forgive myself for being so judgmental and her for being so narcissistic. I tried changing my behavior towards her, acting nice and pretending I liked her. But it was plastic. In my heart, I continued my judgments and never could stop disliking her, or myself.

After petitioning my Higher Self for help, I had a real revelation, one that changed everything and showed me why I couldn't forgive her and showed me how to forgive us both. The information popped into my head in the form of the two critical truths above: 1) The person I didn't like was me. 2) I couldn't forgive myself because I'd been trying to change my behavior rather than change the thoughts that created that behavior. I'd been working at the level of effect rather than at the level of cause.

I saw Paula as an exaggerated form of myself. I'd been projecting my guilt over my own behavior and my dislike of myself onto her. Then, feeling guilty about it, I tried to fix it by forgiving the narcissism, rather than forgiving the thought that caused me to judge her as narcissistic, the thought that I was the guilty party, the indulgent one. I'd been doing everything backwards—which is what the ego mind does in its constant confusion.

I was much more friendly and down to earth than Paula, but I, like Paula, would not allow myself an extra ounce, spending a lot of time jogging and doing high-impact aerobics to remain slender. I too paid careful attention to my clothes and kept my hair perfect. What kind of thoughts or beliefs did I have unconsciously stored that would influence me to be so judgmental of myself? Was I wrong about how I cared for myself? Where did these ideas of right and wrong come from anyway? I had to answer those questions to forgive the thought that created my self-judgments.

Finding Hidden Truths—A Template to Use

I went back to my childhood to uncover any issues I had about clothes and remembered how guilty I'd always felt for wanting and having nice clothes. I remembered hiding anything I bought for a week or two before I brought it out to wear. I needed time to brace myself for the guilt trip I'd encounter when my mother began her lecture telling me how selfish I was. This happened every time I bought anything for myself, even though I always bought clothes with money I'd earned.

With that realization, instead of judging my mother, I began to wonder why my mother felt that it was so wrong for me to buy anything for myself, and why she didn't buy much for herself either. Then I remembered her telling me a story about living through the Great Depression, which hit when she was a young woman and sucked the life right out of her father's business. While she was fortunate enough to get a job in the big city, she had to send her money back to her family to help support them. During those times, it would have been selfish for *her* to buy extra clothes instead of helping her family members who needed the necessities of life.

But, I reasoned, I was not living in a depression. I was living in the happy days when life was good and my father's business was good. Although we weren't wealthy, we wanted for nothing and my family didn't need my financial help. Why did I feel so guilty? My friends expected their parents to buy their clothes, and they did. I'd never expected my parents to provide anything except food and shelter. *Was I really so selfish that I needed to hate myself for spending money to keep myself looking nice? Was my mother right about me?*

I thought about it for quite some time, trying to be as honest with myself as possible. I concluded that I had nothing to feel guilty about. If my family had needed my money, I'd have willingly given up buying clothes. My guilt stemmed from accepting my mother's Depression-induced values as my own, which caused me to become unnecessarily judgmental of myself and guilty for no valid reason.

Next I began to rethink how I was spending money on clothes in the present day. I realized again I was being unnecessarily judgmental of myself. Really, I hadn't had all that many clothes most of my married life. Those I had, I made myself. I'd raised eight children and most of our resources went for their needs. I'd rarely bought anything in the store until I inherited some money, and then I did overindulge for a year or so.

If any of my friends had done the same thing I have said, "Good for you, girl!" You deserve that and more after your thirty-plus years of working eighteen-hour days cooking, cleaning, sewing, car-pooling, bookwork, yard work, caring for the cars, the house, the kids, the husband, helping at his office and in his business, to say nothing of all the church and community work!"

I wouldn't judge my friends as selfish, so why would I judge myself as selfish? After reasoning this through logically rather than thinking with my unconscious programming, I realized I had no reason to feel any guilt about buying clothes. If there was anything to feel guilty about, it was for being too immature, lazy or scared to determine my own values, or at least think through the ones I'd already formed to determine if they were healthy and viable for me. Instead I'd accepted my mother's beliefs as my own without even thinking.

She'd clung to her old depression beliefs and passed them on to her children without even thinking. They weren't my values; they may not have been her real values if she'd thought about it. And they weren't healthy values for my generation. I didn't have to buy into them any longer! I no longer had to feel guilty! I could stop judging myself and give up the guilt over clothes syndrome. I was finally free! I could now easily stop judging myself. As a result, my negative judgments about Paula just melted away and with no effort.

Having resolved my guilt and having forgiven myself, I had nothing to project onto Paula, and we became friends. I found her to be a very lovely person, though a bit insecure; her clothes were compensation for lack of real self-esteem. I had totally misjudged her. *All judgment is misjudgment because it comes from ego, because for ego never sees clearly.* Having rethought all the issues around the guilt over clothes and allowing my behaviors to change, I became much more clear on what I had to forgive.

- I had to forgive myself for thinking I had to take on my mother's beliefs, or anyone else's, without thinking them through.
- I had to forgive myself for thinking I was guilty.
- I had to forgive myself for thinking it was my neighbor who had the problem instead of recognizing the problem was mine, one I'd created from my unexamined thinking.

Once I did that, I felt lighter, clearer, and more connected to the real me. I became ever more grateful for this process of forgiveness. And I was grateful to Paula, whose "narcissistic" behaviors brought up my own hidden guilt and made me face my own destructive thinking patterns that produced my judgmental behaviors. The process worked because I had worked at the level of cause (thought) and watched the effect (behavior) automatically disappear. My story began with how much I disliked my neighbor and it ended with me genuinely liking her. Forgiveness unites.

But it can do much more at a deeper level we don't fully comprehend.

Genuine Forgiveness: A Deep, Mystical Process

There is something very metaphysical about this whole forgiveness process that I wish I could put into words, but complete understanding comes through experience. While doing my forgiveness work recently, I had a brief experience with something incredible and mystical; I experienced a sense of joy and peace and well-being unlike I had never felt before. It became a validation of the power of this forgiveness, a motivation to continue the work of unveiling and exposing all the hidden guilt and judgment in my Pandora's box. These furies are usually brought forth by a negative interaction with another person. Spouses are most valuable in bringing up negative feelings, which we can use to examine our own projections, to forgive and free ourselves.

Because this new forgiveness is such a mystical experience, I can explain it best with mystical, metaphysical information. I'll share the following information from mystics Babaji and Gary Renard mixed with my own inspiration and experiences. For those who are ready, here goes…

Life Is for Giving and Receiving Love

Here's what the gentle mystic teacher Babaji, who teaches big concepts with little words, has to say about forgiving. He tells us that life is for *giving* and for *receiving* love. He tells us that everything in creation is made of love when reduced to its lowest common denominator. He further explains that love connects everything. Babaji believes that Love is the unified field which Einstein was looking for, the common denominator behind all creation. Babaji explains that…

[Love] is the sweet syrup God used to brew everything we ever have or ever will perceive. Love is everything. And we are made to taste of love. That is what our life is for—to receive creation's love. This little concept spells out the misunderstood concept of forgiving.

Grudges are really easy to release when you once realize what a silly illusion they are. You hold grudges because you imagine someone has hurt you. You think you've been attacked, compromised, trespassed, and in some way made a lesser person. Or you imagine someone has taken something from you. Such folly! You are made in the image of God. You are perfection and nothing, no one, can alter that. You are abundance, everything is yours, and all you need comes to you when you open yourself to it. You're truly a creator. You create whatever you experience, if you imagine that someone has hurt you. If you imagine that you have been hurt by anyone, it is only because that is what you as creator, invited.

When you hold grudges, you are choosing to withhold that sweet taste of love you can give. Get rid of the grudge and your life is once again for giving love.

This is a difficult concept to grasp when all of what we call "reality" seems to point in the opposite direction. Our experience seems to indicate that the world is full of mean people preying on the innocent ones. It is so difficult to grasp that this is not so, that we are responsible for our own experiences, creating them either consciously or unconsciously. It may be even harder to grasp that no one can interfere with you and that no one ever has interfered with you. God himself will not interfere with your free will; it is a protected, holy right. While hard to grasp, once it is truly grasped, it will set you free.

Babaji further explains:

You can create whatever you want because you create whatever you think. This wonderful Universe began with God's thought. Likewise our creation begins with our thoughts. In our world of many individual creations—many for each person—we are all actors for each other's script. You are the writer, director, producer and lead character for your script. Everyone else plays in your creation exactly as you direct.

Do you see how powerful you are? Any thought that implies otherwise is an illusion. When you realize the people you hold grudges against are actors in your own creation, they are easy to forgive. Then life is for giving love. This may be one of the truths that may shake you up before it sets you free.

Instead of the old kind of forgiveness we witnessed with Patrick and Paul (which is not forgiveness at all), Babaji suggests the following.

Babaji's Forgiveness Formula

I have made a mistake in my thinking to allow you to seemingly hurt me. I recognize you are merely doing what I invited and that in reality neither you nor anyone can hurt me. I am perfect now, always have been and always will be. You can't change that. I now recognize that life is for giving love to you.

Make this a daily practice, especially whenever you think someone has offended you. At night ask your higher self to feed you the names of those people you need to forgive. Forgive again, and then send love.

Mystic Gary Renard explains that if you're genuinely practicing forgiveness, the Holy Spirit is healing your mind at the level of the unconscious. So you keep going and forgive again and again, even if you have to forgive the same thought that created the behavior over and over because sometimes it is layers deep. *Every time you forgive, something changes in you, even though at first the changes will be unnoticeable to your conscious mind. The changes are happening at a deep level, as more and more layers of curtains are being peeled away. Eventually you'll be able to know the working of this new world.* More on that shortly.

While practicing forgiveness, it works best if you keep it in the forefront of your mind. Even if you feel little irritations, try to isolate the thought that created the irritation and immediately forgive those "little things" as well as the big things, for truly there are no "little things." There are no levels when it comes to forgiveness. There are no levels, period, in 99% thinking.

Maybe you're watching TV and see the cleanup efforts in Haiti after the 2010 earthquake and you're irritated that the relief efforts aren't more organized. Forgive the judgment thought and understand that you don't understand the whole picture and do not have enough information to judge. Then replace the judgment thought with something positive: "It's wonderful how many counties and individuals are concerned over Haiti and are there to help." As you do this, another layer of guilt is peeled away, even if you think nothing is happening.

Going deeper: Renard explains that as you are doing forgiveness work, the Holy Spirit is shining your forgiveness everywhere throughout the mind…It cuts through unconscious guilt and its projections of karma like a laser beam.

That beam pierces all of your past lives, all of your future lives, all through the different dimensions of time, everywhere in the universe of energy and form and through every parallel universe that appears to exist. Incredible things are happening! The Holy Spirit is collapsing time as you sit there. By practicing forgiveness, lessons that we came to learn are erased from this movie we call our life, for we no longer need them. Then all that is left is love, your 99% world of light. In Renard's words:

Every act of forgiveness undoes the ego, and the Holy Spirit removes the blocks to the awareness of God, or spirit's presence. The blocks are those walls of guilt in the mind that keep you from your awareness of what you really are.

Here are suggestions for undoing ego through forgiveness, of both yourself and others.

Renard's Suggestions for Forgiving Yourself

I am immortal spirit. This body is just an image. It has nothing to do with what I really am. I forgive myself for all my misperceptions and judgments and for thinking someone else is guilty, or that I am guilty.

God (higher self, spirit, the universe) is the love in which I forgive myself.

Renard's Suggestions for Forgiving Others

You (name of person you're forgiving) are spirit, whole and innocent. All is forgiven and released.

Use either Babaji's or Renard's suggestions for forgiving, or use them both. Use whatever feels right for you. At first you won't notice a difference because there are so many layers of veils, but eventually you begin feeling different.

Two Ways to Tell Forgiveness Is Working

- You will begin to have periods of feeling very peaceful, although at first they may be very short.

- Things that happen, which once made you feel bad, no longer bother you.

It is through forgiveness that we find our way back home.

Let's review the two essential perspectives to keep in mind that will assist you in your forgiveness work.

Perspective One: No one is doing anything to you that you didn't want to happen. When you are thinking in your 99% mind, you understand that before you came here, you decided what experiences you needed here for your growth and you programmed these experiences into this movie you call your life.

Perspective Two: We created our lives with antagonists—intentionally. If we view this perspective with our 99% mind, we'll see we created them to reveal our own unconscious, repressed guilt so we can heal it, as happened in the case of the clothing judgments.

Your 99% self understands that bringing up and releasing repressed guilt through forgiveness is the fastest way to move from the world of fear to the world of love and find your real self. I have said it before, and will continue to say it in many different ways, for this concept is of paramount importance if you are to find the real you.

The reason forgiveness is the way out of the 1% ego world is because love and fear can't be in the same place at the same time. You can't be in your 99% world of love when you are harboring resentments and anger, which are created from fear. Once we let go of fear, we are freed to give and receive love in its many and various forms, to be like our creator.

Before we can find the Truth we thirst after, we need to find our way out of this ego-world maze of illusions, a world so complicated we can hardly see anything beyond it. The more I was able to drop the illusions, the simpler the path became as I recognized these truths:

- All there is, is Love and Fear.
- Love has its own thought system (99% thinking).
- Fear has its own thought system (1% thinking).
- Everything is created by thought.
- What we create is determined by what thought system we're using.
- What we create from love thoughts always produces positive results and moves us out of this world of illusion.
- What we create from fear thoughts always produces negative results, which keep us stuck in the 1% world of illusions.

This is the perspective of the mystic.

Is It Love, or Fear?

If we are not acting out of love, we are acting out of fear.

This explains why forgiveness is so necessary, because love and fear cannot exist in the same place at the same time. I'll remind you again, if you are tuned into the AM FEAR station, you can't, at the same time be tuned into the FM LOVE station. To reach the FM LOVE station, we must be vibrating at that frequency, meaning we must get out of fear and erase our fearful negative thoughts that keep us stuck there. This is accomplished by the technology of true forgiveness.

That is what forgiveness is for. Through forgiveness, we can escape our fear-based 1% world and find our 99% world where we can give and receive genuine love. Our 99% world is a world of love and peace.

Caution: The ego will interpret love as chemistry and sex, because the ego doesn't understand that love is ubiquitous and can take many forms. Our 99% mind knows at the deepest level, we all love each other deeply; it knows how to manifest love in the most appropriate manner in each individual circumstance. The ego, living in fear, will never understand true love.

> *Forgiveness is the great need of this world, but that is because...*
> *[we live in] a world of illusions. Those who forgive are thus releasing*
> *themselves from illusions, while those who withhold forgiveness are*
> *binding themselves to them.*
>
> *Condemn and you are made a prisoner. Forgive and you are*
> *made free.*
>
> —From *A Course in Miracles*

> *And leave a path for others to follow you to the 99% world, where*
> *they too can find their real powerful Selves.*

I've given you some very practical reasons for forgiving, some very esoteric reasons for forgiving, and some ways to help you forgive. I've even left you with ideas on how forgiveness works at a metaphysical level. But here's one more thing I leave you with...a choice. Will you now begin practicing forgiveness?

Your decision is important because the world will never have peace until the individuals in the world have inner peace, for what is happening in the world is simply an outward manifestation of the collective thoughts of those who live here.

Individuals will never have peace until they learn and practice the new forgiveness. Your decision affects the world.

After that, where does forgiveness ultimately take us? When every trace of guilt is removed from your unconscious mind, you will break the cycle of birth and death according to the mystics. And then what?

Who but a mystic could answer that question, and who but a mystic who has experienced the "then what" could answer it most accurately? Thus I share with you, the experience of mystic Gary Renard.

Suddenly I felt weightless as my body disappeared. There was nothing to see, only an experience of total awareness. The ecstasy of what I was experiencing was beyond words. It was the experience of revelation and I had been within it before, but this time the awareness of my body wasn't returning, and I didn't know if I could stand the joy. In the wholeness of this experience, everyone was there whom I had ever loved—not as bodies, not as separate things, but in my awareness of perfect oneness.

He explains that every animal, every friend, every relative, anyone he'd cared for or loved was there. Even his mystical teachers, Arten and Pursah, were there and he knew then that he would not miss them when they were gone, as he had always feared, for their unlimited love extended through eternity. He explained that the joy of this reality exceeded every expectation he might have had. He said, "In the all-encompassing wonder of God, there was no need to think, only to love only to be what I really am."

After this timeless experience, he explains that he was once again sitting in his chair, seemingly in a body.

I heard the Voice of the Holy Spirit, full and whole, and I knew it was my voice, the voice of Arten and Pursah, the voice of Jesus and

Buddha the Voice of All in One. As I listened to the message, I closed my eyes and heard these words:

Each day that you forgive, the effects of all the world's mistakes are melted as snow into a burning fire. No more guilt, no more karma, no more fear of what may be, For you have met yourself and declared your innocence, and all that follows is as natural as God.

Reynard further explained that our old ideas of birth and death were just that—ideas. If we were to come again, it would be to help a few more people, but even if we came as a body, that's not the real us, the real us is…love. In his own words:

The day will come when pain is impossible, love is everywhere, and truth is all there is. You've longed for this forever often silently and without knowing it. The knowledge of what you are is more certain now, and love has forgotten no one…the day will come when there is nothing left to forgive, and celebration with your sisters and brothers is in order. And then the day will come when there is no more need for days. And you will live as one forever in the holiness of your immortal reality.

Love forgives; only fear condemns.

Forgiveness then undoes what fear has produced; returning the mind to the awareness of God [whatever it is to you]. For this reason, forgiveness can truly be called salvation. It is the means by which illusions disappear.

—From *A Course in Miracles*

SUMMING IT UP

The Mystic's Perspective

Through your forgiveness does the truth about yourself return to your memory...
Do you not then begin to understand what forgiveness will do for you? It will take away all fear and guilt and pain. It will restore the invulnerability and power God gave His son to your awareness.
—From *A Course in Miracles Workbook*

The world we once called real—*the one we access with our five senses—we've identified as our 1% world, for that is where you find 1% of truth. We called the other world, the 99% world, for that is where you find 99% of truth. The truth is what sets us free. The 99% world is the world of the mystic. It is also the world where genuine forgiveness takes place.*

The following is a review of the characteristics of each world:

233

1%	99%
• We experience spiritual darkness and confusion.	• We are surrounded by order, perfection and light.
• We're caught up in the ego world— never feeling good enough.	• We are confident and humble.
• We are victims of circumstances and have no control.	• We are victors with total control.
• We feel empty, unfulfilled, turn to addictions.	• We are fulfilled, in the *genuine* us.
• We unconsciously create what we don't want.	• We consciously create what we desire.
• There is no hope for permanent, positive change.	• We can create permanent, lasting change.
• We create problems.	• We solve problems.
• Our fear-based thought system rules	• Our love-based thought system takes over.
• Pain is dominant.	• Peace reigns.

Einstein referred to these two worlds when he said, "The significant problems we face cannot be solved at the same level of thinking we were at when we created them." The thought system each world has helps create and maintain that world. The world where we create our problems we've called the 1% world. We've called the world where you solve them the 99% world. Finding our way from one to the other really is the solution to everything.

This has been our journey.

"But," you say," I'm not there yet."

None of us are all the time, but now there's a map to refer to when you get lost. It is a journey, not a destination. Inch by inch, yard by yard, and sometimes mile by mile we get ever closer to our goal, then we take a few steps into that world and ego pulls us back, but we recover and continue to march forward again. It's the only true way to genuine peace and joy. Although ego will tell us instant gratification is the way to go; it's not. I've shared the signs that tell you that you are making progress on your evolutionary path and the benefits you'll experience. We'll review them again shortly.

APPENDIX:

Found at <u>www.RisingFromAshes.net</u> Code: *rising*.

To keep this book at a manageable length, I've posted source material and other information on my website that will take intellectually curious readers deeper into some of the more important concepts covered. Here you will find several articles that analyze some of the book's topics in more depth:

- *Special Report: Are You the Next Target of a Con Artist:* This explains the kind of people who are likely to be conned, how to not remain a victim if you have been conned, the psychological symptoms victims experience and how con men con.

- *How to Avoid the Nation's Top Scams*: The top scams from 2010 are worth hanging onto since they are not likely to disappear in 2011. Some are novel, but most are golden oldies—time-tested rip-offs with a new twist that cruelly capitalizes on people's current financial distress.

- *Analysis of Nathaniel Hawthorne's short story "The Birthmark":* This is included for it is a sophisticated story of how people confuse love for addiction and the damage it does to a marriage and each individual in it. This error is more common that we'd like to believe.

- *Analysis of the Language of Good and Evil:* This rare information comes from a yet-to-be published doctoral thesis. Much of what was learned came from interviews with Satan worshippers and how they suck victims into their covens.

EPILOGUE

When I began this book, I wondered how to best motivate people to take on the task of discovering who they really are when we've become an indulgent society programmed to seek instant gratification. Consider how we're programmed with suggestions like this one, printed in four luscious colors, sitting on every order counter of a nationwide restaurant chain…"Eat Dessert First."

"The task seems so overwhelming!" Yikes, my ego thoughts are popping up again.

Then I listened to my wiser voice, "Now is the time. People are ready for change, for everything in their old world is breaking down—the economic system, the social system, and the political system. They are looking for answers, ways to survive. You are teaching them not only to survive but how they can thrive in any adversity."

My wiser self continued, "People are tired of war, both their inner and outer wars; they want peace and don't know how to get it. You know, and everyone else needs to know, that if we are ever to have peace out there, we need to first create peace inside ourselves. For the 'out there world' is only a reflection of what goes on in our 'in here' worlds."

Then a thought popped into my head, one that came from a conversation I'd had years before with some friends. It caused me to see an even more critical need for a book that would encourage and help people find their lost and powerful selves. The conversation centered on personal transformation and the evolution of consciousness. Someone mentioned a scientific study done on a tiny island near Japan in the 1960s. It came to be known as the 100th monkey effect.

The 100th Monkey

Curious, I did research to find out more. I learned that on a small island near Japan, a group of scientists was studying the monkeys who lived there. They began feeding them sweet potatoes and observing their behavior.

One monkey began taking the sweet potatoes to the ocean to wash the sand off before he ate them. Then, in twos and threes, more monkeys decided to do the same. Then suddenly, after what they estimated to be the 100th monkey washed his sweet potato, the whole island of monkeys began the same behavior *all at once*. Even more surprising, all the monkeys on an island many miles way soon began to show the same behavior, all at once.

Some scientists involved in the experiment wouldn't acknowledge their involvement because the results weren't measurable with their current scientific methods; they were afraid of losing credibility in the scientific community. Other accounts of the 100th Monkey study suggest that the change took place over a period of years, and that some older monkeys never did change while most of the younger monkeys did. Now that the new science of quantum physics has produced a way to validate the experiment, I hope someone repeats it.

Some people use the experiment as a metaphor to explain Rupert Sheldrake's scientific concept of morphic fields and morphic resonance. This concept is simply another way of describing a collective unconscious where like energies collect, connect, become stronger and powerfully influence the collective whole. While the accounts of the 100th Monkey differ in details, none of them question this collective energy field, or that like energies collect and connect, and that the more of that collective energy there is, the more powerfully it influences the whole.

What does this mean to us? Simply that the more people who practice this thought-energy work, the more we assist the transformation of this planet to a kinder, gentler place. We don't know if the final transformation will be spontaneous when we reach a critical mass of this consciousness, or whether it will take place gradually over time. But evidence suggests that we will indeed influence this global transformation, and that influence begins with our own transformation.

As I recalled the monkeys, I remembered something I'd read in Owen Waters' book, *The Shift: The Revolution in Human Consciousness,* where he explained that this transformation wasn't unique to monkeys:

> *This transformation of consciousness, the greatest one ever recorded, first became apparent in the mid-1960s and has been building momentum ever since.*

> *The Shift is a collective transformation consisting of the sum of the steps each individual makes to step into the New Reality. [99% thinking] Each person, in their own time, is moving forward into a stage of consciousness, which brings a wider vista and an awareness that springs from the heart. When enough people's primary attention becomes focused through their hearts, then the "hundredth monkey effect" will occur.*

Writer and spiritual teacher Eckhart Tolle tells us that if we as a people are going to assist this transformation, we must learn to use our minds effectively, instead of letting our minds use us. I quote...

The mind is a superb instrument if used rightly. Used wrongly, however, it becomes very destructive. To put it more accurately, it is not so much that you use your mind wrongly—you usually don't use it at all. It uses you. This is the disease.

Then Tolle sounds a louder alarm:

When faced with a radical crisis, when the old way of [thinking and] being in the world, of interacting with each other and with the realm of nature doesn't work anymore, when survival is threatened by seemingly insurmountable problems, an individual life form—or species will either die or become extinct OR rise above the limitation of the condition through an evolutionary leap.

The evolutionary leap is to find that new thought system Einstein speaks about—our 99% thought system—the one that allows us to see beyond our five senses and permanently solve our problems.

When we take the evolutionary leap, we become part of the group of the conscious people who have found their real powerful selves, those who contribute positively to the group consciousness and transformation of the planet.

Do It Anyway

Again my 1% voice takes over and says, "This is an awesome task to try and help the reader take the evolutionary leap. Are you sure you can do this? Are you sure you want to?" Then it answered its own question, saying, "You don't *really* want to do this!"

As the 1% voice shouted in my ears, I shut it off long enough to hear a faint but powerful whisper…"Do it anyway!" Then I understood it was not me who would convince anyone of anything. All I could do was point out the path to their 99% world where all truth lies, that is where the convincing would take place. There they recognize who they really are.

Have you yet discovered your 99% self, even for a moment? Have you recognized, even for moment, how powerful you are? *Do you realize you've always been a creator? Is it now clear that when our minds live in the 1% world of ego, you create out of your conscious or unconscious fears and that fear based thinking eventually brings negative results? Is it now clear that when you move to your 99% world, you create consciously out of love and create positive results?*

Can you fully comprehend the ability you have to create your life, as you would like it—if you are willing do the work to remove the barriers that separate you from your real, powerful self? Does the thought scare you or does it not even compute? Does the responsibility and/or work overwhelm you? I surely understand that, but you have the power and ability so…Do it anyway!

When we first contact our 99% selves, it likely won't last long but that's where we all start—making contact for a moment, then increasing the time as we continue to remove the barriers that keep us separated from our real selves.

Will we sometimes fail?

Yes, but we will simply

Try again.

Will we forget who we really are?

Yes, but then

We will remember and

Try again!

Then

Little by little

We'll find ourselves being

Less concerned about

Things that once concerned us.

And

We'll feel more

And more at peace.

As we continue to walk through our

1% world fears

We'll find on the other side

The 99% world of Love

Where

We begin creating our *true* desires

With only a thought . . .

And we'll know we have mastered

The Phoenix Principle

And we'll know

The prize is worth the price.

A VISUAL SUMMARY OF
RISING FROM ASHES

This is where the book began…in a world of chaos.

Chaos *

To get an image of how the book can end, do the following:

Relax and concentrate on the four dots on the image for 30 to 40 seconds.

Then look at a wall near you (any smooth, single-colored surface).

You will see a circle of light developing.

Start blinking your eyes a couple of times and you will see a figure emerging. What do you see, or whom do you see?

Do you think it is an image of Jesus? It isn't. It is an image of you. It is an image of your internal guru, the Christ in you, the real you. This has been our journey of discovery.

Christ

Everyone has a divine being within waiting to be acknowledged—Jews, Muslims, Christians, Buddhists and atheists. Mystics would call it your God self, or your 99% self, others would call it your higher self. Metaphysical churches sometimes refer to that divine being as the Christ within.

We find our Christ within as we remove the barriers that stand between our divine nature and the ego driven us. As we do, we earn the divine privilege of watching the doors of our 99% world begin to swing wide open, and we're invited in to discover this wonderful new world.

Jesus the Christ (Jesus is the man, Christ is a title) put it this way:

He that believeth on me, the works that I do shall he do also; and greater works than these shall he do —John 14:12

These great works we'll do can happen after we've entered this wonderful new 99% world and mastered its way of thinking. While the "great works" originate in the 99% world of thought, they manifest in our 1% world.

How am I doing at stretching your old belief system? Do you feel like hiding back in your old ideas?

I know it's difficult to believe you have this kind of power, but you do. I warned you that this book would challenge your thinking. But remember the blessings that came to the Senegalese Muslims when they challenged their old belief system.

Wake up and *remember* who you are!

---

* Thanks to those at Yahoo! mail for the image

NOTE TO THE READER:

I have spent many years, many dollars and many sleepless nights working to get this message right for you.

I ask you to consider doing one thing for me…

Pay It Forward.

And

Do not go where the wide, 1% superhighway may lead.

Choose instead to travel the narrow, 99% road, the Road Less Traveled

Then go where there is no superhighway, or road

And, using your 99% mind, create a path for others to follow.

And

Stand up on the inside. You now know how.

RECLAIMER*

In a conversation with God, a young child, who had not yet come to earth, discovered…he was light.

But, he wanted to *feel* what it was like to be the light.

God said, *"Since you cannot see yourself as the light when you are in the Light, we'll surround you with darkness."*

"What's darkness?" the Little Soul asked.

God replied, **"It is what you are not."**

"Will I be afraid of the dark," cried The Little Soul.

"Only if you choose to be," God answered.

"In order to experience anything at all, the exact opposite will appear…It is a great gift," God said, *"because without it, you could not know what anything is like."*

Adapted from *"The Little Soul and the Sun"*
By **Neale Donald Walsch**

• Reclaim here means: To bring back to memory the truth of what is and what we are.

"Murder, Death and Rebirth:
What I Learned from Murder"

by Claudia T. Nelson

A true story that began near a gracefully flowing river set amidst the pines and aspens at a cabin called Tiede's Tranquility, named after the author's sister, Kaye Tiede who owned it.

But tranquility would turn to terror... three days before the Christmas of 1990. What happened on that day, at that cabin, shocked a nation and traumatized a family for decades.

It has dominated the author's thinking, and actions for over twenty years. *Murder, Death and Rebirth* is the result. In *Murder, Death and Rebirth* the author shares her story of trauma and healing, leaving the reader with startling, life enhancing insights.

**Book will be available for a download on December 1, 2011 for $5.00
at ClaudiaNelson.com**

BUY A SHARE OF THE FUTURE IN YOUR COMMUNITY

These certificates make great holiday, graduation and birthday gifts that can be personalized with the recipient's name. The cost of one S.H.A.R.E. or one square foot is $54.17. The personalized certificate is suitable for framing and will state the number of shares purchased and the amount of each share, as well as the recipient's name. The home that you participate in "building" will last for many years and will continue to grow in value.

THIS CERTIFIES THAT

YOUR NAME HERE

HAS INVESTED IN A HOME FOR A DESERVING FAMILY

1985-2010

TWENTY-FIVE YEARS OF BUILDING FUTURES
IN OUR COMMUNITY ONE HOME AT A TIME

1200 SQUARE FOOT HOUSE @ $65,000 = $54.17 PER SQUARE FOOT
This certificate represents a tax deductible donation. It has no cash value.

Here is a sample SHARE certificate:

YES, I WOULD LIKE TO HELP!

I support the work that Habitat for Humanity does and I want to be part of the excitement! As a donor, I will receive periodic updates on your construction activities but, more importantly, I know my gift will help a family in our community realize the dream of homeownership. **I would like to SHARE in your efforts against substandard housing in my community!** *(Please print below)*

PLEASE SEND ME _____ SHARES at $54.17 EACH = $ $_____

In Honor Of: _____

Occasion: (Circle One)   HOLIDAY   BIRTHDAY   ANNIVERSARY

OTHER: _____

Address of Recipient: _____

Gift From: _____ *Donor Address:* _____

Donor Email: _____

I AM ENCLOSING A CHECK FOR $ $_____ PAYABLE TO HABITAT FOR HUMANITY **OR** PLEASE CHARGE MY VISA OR MASTERCARD *(CIRCLE ONE)*

Card Number _____ Expiration Date: _____

Name as it appears on Credit Card _____ Charge Amount $ _____

Signature _____

Billing Address _____

Telephone # Day _____ Eve _____

PLEASE NOTE: Your contribution is tax-deductible to the fullest extent allowed by law.
Habitat for Humanity • P.O. Box 1443 • Newport News, VA 23601 • 757-596-5553
www.HelpHabitatforHumanity.org

Printed in the USA
CPSIA information can be obtained
at www.ICGtesting.com
JSHW082157140824
68134JS00014B/278

9 781600 379963